SEARCHING FOR DOT LEMON

MYSTERY WOMAN-WHO WAS SHE

RICHARD KINSMAN

outskirts
press

To Anna,

Love,

Gramps

This book is dedicated to those unfortunate orphaned children without identified natural parents, who often must develop their own individual self identities.

May 2019

Table of Contents

Prologue

WHO KNEW THAT my posting to the US Embassy, Venezuela in 1971 would lead me on a near lifelong quest to discover the truth, or truths, about Dot Lemon. She was a foundling who grew up to become an immensely talented woman, deserving to be listed among the outstanding female characters and aviators of the 20th century. The enigmas and somewhat mystical secrecy of her life story form a labyrinth, yet through assembled facts, a fascinating passage into the pages of history of an undiscovered female heroic figure named Dot Lemon.

CHAPTER 1

Caracas, Venezuela

Who is she?

AS A NEWLY arrived consular officer at the US Embassy in 1971, I was assigned duties of "Protection and Welfare," broadly defined as looking out for the well-being of US citizens in Venezuela who encountered difficulties of one sort or another.

My impromptu and unanticipated introduction to Dot Lemon arrived in the form of a phone call the first day in my new office. After I said hello, the woman on the other side of the line began a mostly stream of consciousness monologue which made little sense to me, and left me wondering if I was the intended contact. After some difficulty I finally managed to end the call as gracefully as possible, given that I had no idea who the caller may have been and not wishing to offend anyone. This did not seem an auspicious beginning to my new assignment. Who was this unknown caller? Looking for my predecessor, who was to leave shortly for his next assignment, I mentioned this rather strange phone call from the unidentified woman.

With a somewhat malevolent grin, he described an emaciated sixty-four-year-old US citizen woman with wispy brilliant red hair, legally blind, occasionally somewhat confused, and in overall frail health. She had become a de facto ward of the

Embassy Consular Section, and more importantly, as I would quickly learn, she was now to be my responsibility. Her name was Dot Lemon, truth at that time, and the only established fact about her that I would have for a long time.

In 1971 I could never have imagined how my efforts to plumb the history, origins, career, and motivation of this incredible woman would occupy and frustrate me for so many years. The real search began some years later, but in the meantime Dot became my professional consular responsibility as a US citizen who needed, and demanded, lots of attention.

She would quickly move to the top of my consular responsibilities list, as a long-time US citizen resident in Venezuela, suffering mental and physical disabilities, as well as financial problems. Her Spanish was rudimentary; she described to me being victimized by a number of avaricious Venezuelan lawyers and confidence men, of whom there was no shortage, added to by her often confused mental state of imagined pursuit by nefarious criminal organizations. This was very much an unanticipated complication to my role as a Consular official, as well as a totally unimagined beginning of my pursuit of the life story of Dot.

Dot continued her phone conversations with me, virtually every day. She would usually call around 11 a.m., to continue a monologue about her living, eating, and survival efforts. Sometime around noon I would place the phone receiver on my desk and leave for lunch. She didn't require much input or conversation from me, and would invariably be there still talking when I returned thirty or forty-five minutes later.

Lest the reader form a mistaken impression of my opinion of the lady, I in fact became fascinated by her and concerned about her welfare. She had many appealing and surprising qualities, among which was a deep interest, belief in, and practice of astronomy and astrology. She frequently astonished me by accurately citing biographic facts of my parents and me, based on astrology. She had questioned me about my life and date of birth. We were both Leos, which meant a lot to her.

Her daily life was a struggle, and she quickly became my most time-consuming consular responsibility. The real irony of this situation was that consular duties were only my day job. My real job was as a career officer of another United States Government Agency. Nevertheless, Dot required considerable care and even feeding such as when I took her to lunch at a corner restaurant. This allowed me to see her, once a stranger, as a very needy complicated individual, leading to her becoming an informal ward of mine in my role as a Consular officer. Subsequently, I bought her a gift of a hot plate which she more than once told me had saved her life.

One night, at home and sound asleep, I received a phone call at 4:30 a.m. Fearing the worst, I struggled to clear my brain. I picked up the phone, and without preamble, the caller said, "Look out the window, your planets are perfectly aligned." It was, of course, Dot!

She also presented me with an inscribed copy of her book entitled One One, an allegorical tale of "The Life, Death and the Resurrection of an Airplane." Her inscription to me reads: "To Dick Kinsman—A Leo Who Understands Another One. With the Greatest of Best Wishes to Him and His. Xmas 1972, Caracas, Venezuela."[1]

It only occurred to me some years later to really question why Dot was so alone in Venezuela, and how she ended up there without apparent help from friends or family. I knew she had some vague connection to gold mining interests, but my knowledge ended there, given my overriding professional and personal concerns about her personal welfare, and my real career. At that time I never imagined what events and complications her life story would reveal to me. She was resolute, but obviously had struggled in her day-to-day existence at this time in her life. She did not then give any indication of her previous

To

Dick Kinsman — A Leo
who understands another one.
With the greatest of best
wishes to Him and His —

Dot Lemon

Xmas 1972
Caracas Venezuela —

Dot Lemon Book Inscription to Author

heroic accomplishments as an aviator, author, navigator, and gold mine owner. My subsequent discoveries of her incredible life, prior to our friendship from 1971-73, unfortunately occurred many years later after her death in 1986, greatly complicating my later efforts to uncover sources.

But at that particular time while I was a Consular Officer in Venezuela, she was just part of my daily activities that I shared in conversation at home during drinks with my wife. After hearing about Dot for many weeks, my wife suggested that we invite her to dinner at our home. Dot always referred to my wife as "Joy," which is not my wife's real name. I was never sure if this was the result of Dot's possibly faulty memory, or perhaps more likely something to do with Dot's astrological talents, in reference to the happy alignment between my wife and me.

Dot turned out to be an accomplished dinner conversationalist, able to discuss music and the theater very knowledgeably. She was much more lucid and sophisticated in this setting, as opposed to her routine morning phone calls to me. She had stories about her royal Danish ancestry, and the many fabulous jewels her father/grandfather had given her. She also mentioned her son "Little Red," who was killed in the Korean War, and three other sons, details of whom would remain obscure. My wife and I never saw any of those jewels, nor did she reveal any specific details of her family, other than a vague reference to a twin brother who died at birth. While seeming to have little relevance at that time to Dot's life story, this detail would later add to the mystery of Dot's birth and origins.

This rather extreme reticence with regard to family and background details seemed to carry through much of my future research regarding her life. Of course at this time in Venezuela I had no idea nor interest in discovering her earlier years, a process that would subsequently prove daunting , and all the more challenging given the passage of some three decades before my research began.

SEARCHING FOR DOT LEMON

Dot was a truly enigmatic woman some of whose biographical details have proven to be hard to pin down. I have made it my pursuit of years to sort through mysterious facts and events surrounding the circumstances of her life to discover this global nomad of uncertain European and American heritage, the aviator of astonishing accomplishments, the entrepreneur in risky gold-mining ventures, and a woman of myriad facets, in every way, always surprising.

CHAPTER **2**

Who was she?

SOME YEARS LATER, thirty-three years to be exact, in 2006, having retired from active USG (US Government) service, I was in the Middle East on a short term TDY (temporary duty) contract with the US military. With long afternoons of little work responsibility, nothing to do, and no place to go as I was in the middle of a desert on a restricted military installation, I began serious internet surfing, starting for no apparent reason with the country of Venezuela.

In retrospect, I now believe some astrological influence by Dot may well have led me back to the place where I met, and became acquainted with her. In short order, on a Venezuelan website, I learned about Jimmie Angel, an American itinerant bush pilot who discovered the world's highest waterfall while searching for gold in Venezuela. "Angel Falls" is named after him. Alongside him in the website photo stood his first wife, a stunning redhead, named Virginia, nee Martin. I was instantly mesmerized, because Angel's wife, Virginia Martin Angel, appeared to be my former Venezuelan consular charge, Dot Lemon. I recognised Angel's wife as apparently Dot, from a photo of her taken circa the 1950's which appeared in Dot Lemon's own book "One-One," a copy of which she had given me in 1971.

Like a revelation, almost an epiphany, it struck me that this Virginia Angel and Dot Lemon were one and the same person. I knew from my days in Caracas, Venezuela that Dot Lemon had flaming red hair, had some connection to gold mining in Venezuela, and had been a pilot. Thus, in addition to the photo likeness, Dot's history seemed to me to mesh with the story of Jimmie Angel, a pilot who had searched for gold in Venezuela.

This startling connection with my old Venezuelan friend after so many years seemed almost providential, leaving me with no choice but to pursue this incredible and coincidental concurrence of identities. Later research showed that Dot's previous surname had indeed been Martin, the maiden name of Jimmie Angel's wife, Virginia Martin. This seemed to reinforce my supposition that Virginia (Martin) Angel and Dot (Martin) Lemon were one and the same person. I was hooked and had to know more. Little did I realize at that time that "wanting to know more" would lead to years of researching and growing fascination with Dot Lemon's life story.

I had never really forgotten Dot after leaving Venezuela in July 1973, having spent much time and effort in those former years on her behalf in my role as Consular officer concerned about her welfare. While I was in Venezuela, she had become a friend, a sympathetic figure, and a memorable character, but now at this time in my life and career, a feature of the past. Dot had not forgotten me either, however, and I received long single spaced letters from her in August 1973, a year after I had left Venezuela, and years later in September 1980.[2]

The 1973 letter, which only caught up with me many weeks later after home leave and reassignment, addressed me as "Dear Comrade Leo Child,"

How nice of you to think of sending me that cheering birthday card. I needed it. The days from 16 August to my birthday the 22nd have become the 6 days of horror for me since the tragedies took place. You, as a Leo know we never forget, we just get control. But I don't seem to have gotten hold of myself yet on this last one. I've wept so much that yesterday and today my whole self just seems to be deadened."

While naturally concerned, I had no idea at that time what "tragedies" she was referring to in this letter, and as my responsibilities for her had passed on to another Consular officer in Venezuela, her tragedies had no context for me. I could only hope that she was in good hands. Later research produced information alluding to plane crashes of a grandson and family, which may have been the tragedies referred to in this letter. However, details of sons and grandsons remain one of her various life story intrigues, and I only later began to learn about yet another aspect of her life - the mystery regarding her four sons.

In this letter of August 1973, she also asked if she had worn a pair of diamond earrings to dinner at our house, citing the three pairs she had had with her in Caracas. Real, or not? This reference to jewelry may be relevant to a letter exchange between Dot and Margaret Weems, dated 24 October 1963 which I discovered in later research.

This Weems letter[3] involved a dispute about diamond bracelets lent to Dot by Margaret Weems, the wife of Admiral Weems (ret), past president of the Institute of Navigation (ION), an organization which becomes a future interlude in Dot's remarkable life story. The letter exchange attempted to settle whether Dot had ever returned the bracelets to Margaret Weems or paid for them. I mention this in reference to Dot's frequent allusion to my wife and me in Caracas regarding fabulous jewelry given to her by her father and grandfather. These claims contrast with her gratitude for having been lent the bracelets, which she should have had no need for given her oft mentioned personal jewelry - which neither my wife nor I had ever seen.

The remainder of six single-spaced typed pages of the letter addressed to me in August 1973 contained her semi-lucid wide-ranging political musings, among which she continued to refer to my wife as "Joy," and to once again acknowledge my having saved her life with the seemingly insignificant gift of a hotplate for heating her meagre meals in 1971/2, the years I had been the Consular officer in Venezuela concerned with her welfare .

The September 1980 letter (six years prior to her death in 1986) ran to twenty-one single-spaced pages. It was obvious that Dot's mental state had further deteriorated, in that sections of the letter alternated between lucid and the apparently delusional.

In 1980, as I had not yet begun my extended effort to re-search and understand her complicated life, I did not make the time to continue our correspondence across distance and time. She was still in Venezuela, while I was pursuing my career as an Intelligence Officer in the Caribbean and in Europe. Dot was sixty-five years old when I knew her in Venezuela, having re-vealed to me no evidence of a prior extraordinary life , aspects of which I would only years later discover.

To my everlasting regret, it was some thirty-three years later, in 2006, well after her 1986 death in Caracas, that I encoun-tered her photograph next to Jimmie Angel, and subsequently became fascinated as details emerged about her life and ac-complishments. Thus there was no opportunity to question her about the later unanswered enigmas of her life. Even if I had known to ask her about these mysteries in 1971-73, I am not sure how she might have responded. My belief, in this regard, rests on the fact that much of her history, and her version of it, has revealed a life story that remains an absorbing combination of fact and fancy.

CHAPTER 3

Marriage—Or Marriages?

AFTER THAT DAY in the Middle East in 2006 when I believed Virginia Angel and Dot Lemon could be the same person, I began an effort to learn more about Virginia Angel (Jimmie Angel's first wife), possibly identified as my old friend Dot Lemon. I was energized by the seeming dual identity issue, and my starting point was research about Virginia (Martin) Angel.

Virginia Martin married Jimmie Angel in August 1922, in Kansas. Virginia was eighteen and Angel twenty-three. She had been a wing-walker and barnstormer when she met Jimmie, who had also barnstormed in the 1920s. Barnstormers were itinerant pilots who toured the country, offering plane rides wherever they could find paying customers, usually in rural small towns. Wing walkers were daredevil individuals, often women, who stood on aircraft wings during flight.

Jimmie and Virginia, nee Martin, were separated in 1933, after which Virginia lived a secluded life in the southwestern part of the United States. They were never legally divorced. She gave no interviews following the separation, and at that stage of my research it still seemed possible to me, even probable, that Virginia may have emerged somewhat later as Dot Lemon. I was consumed by the idea, not really knowing anything about Dot's existence prior to our early 1970s Venezuelan passage. It thus became of primary importance, as the next phase of my research, to know more about Dot previous to my acquaintance with her in Venezuela, and the imagined (by me) morphing of Virginia Martin Angel into the Dot I knew in 1971. To my surprise, a heretofore totally unforeseen life story began to slowly emerge in bits and pieces about thirty-three years after my initial introduction to the dear lady. However, to start with, it turned out that indeed Dot Lemon was probably not Jimmie Angel's wife Virginia, the wing walker, as I once theorized. Not only was Dot probably not ever Jimmie Angel's wife, but Dot's true marriage arrangements provided ever more convoluted threads to her story.

Searching for Dot Lemon in public records revealed that Dot, then named Dorothy C. Brink, married one William Richmond Lemon in Miami, Florida, on 3 April 1937, according to Marriage License 7858, State of Florida, Palm Beach County.[4]

This record was a deceptively simple beginning to her intriguing history, which I puzzled over during long periods of doubt as I attempted to reconstruct events some seventy years after the fact. A new record emerged five years after her recorded legal marriage to William Richmond Lemon in 1937. Dorothy filed an affidavit in Miami, Florida, dated 6 January 1942, stating that she, at that time in 1927 named Dorothy Culver Whitney, had been married to a Leon Brink at Rochester, New York, on 18 October 1927. She further stated, "I obtained a divorce from Brink on 10 March 1937 in West Palm Beach, Florida."[5] She signed this affidavit as "Dorothy C. Lemon." So, in the 1942 affidavit, signed by Dorothy C. Lemon, she states she married Leon Brink in 1927, her maiden name at that time being Dorothy Culver Whitney. Could things become even more tangled?

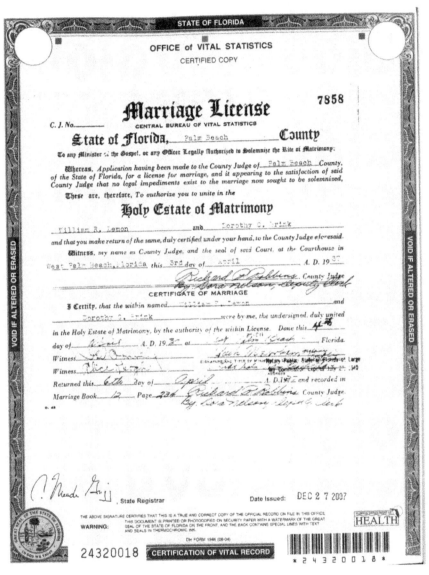

OFFICE of VITAL STATISTICS

CERTIFIED COPY

Marriage License

7858

C. J. No._____

CENTRAL BUREAU OF VITAL STATISTICS

State of Florida, Palm Beach County

To any Minister of the Gospel, or any Officer Legally Authorized to Solemnize the Rite of Matrimony:

Whereas, Application having been made to the County Judge of Palm Beach County, of the State of Florida, for a license for marriage, and it appearing to the satisfaction of said County Judge that no legal impediments exist to the marriage now sought to be solemnized,

These are, therefore, To authorize you to unite in the

Holy Estate of Matrimony

William R. Lemon and Dorothy C. Brink

and that you make return of the same, duly certified under your hand, to the County Judge aforesaid.

Witness, my name as County Judge, and the seal of said Court, at the Courthouse in

West Palm Beach, Florida this 3rd day of April A. D. 19__, County Judge

By _____, Deputy Clerk

CERTIFICATE OF MARRIAGE

I Certify, that the within named William R. Lemon and Dorothy C. Brink were by me, the undersigned, duly united

in the Holy Estate of Matrimony, by the authority of the within License. Done this ____

day of _____ A. D. 19__ at _____ Florida.

Witness _____

Witness _____

Returned this 6th day of April A. D. 19__ and recorded in

Marriage Book 12 Page 234 _____ County Judge.

By _____, Deputy Clerk

o. 48

_____ , State Registrar

Date Issued: DEC 2 7 2007

HEALTH

24320018 CERTIFICATION OF VITAL RECORD *24320018*

Brink/Lemon Marriage License

JANUARY 6
19 42

I, DOROTHY CULVER WHITNEY WAS MARRIED TO LEON BRINK AT ROCHESTER, NEW YORK, IN OCTOBER 18, 1927. I OBTAINED A DIVORCE FROM HIM IN MARCH 1937 IN WEST PALM BEACH, FLORIDA. ON APRIL 4, 1937, I MARRIED WILLIAM RICHMOND LEMON IN WEST PALM BEACH, FLORIDA.

Dorothy C. Lemon

SUBSCRIBED AND SWORN TO BEFORE ME AT MIAMI, FLORIDA THIS 6TH DAY OF JANUARY 1942.

Elizabeth Da...

Notary Public, State of Florida at large,
My commission expires Dec. 2, 1945,
Bonded by Mass. Bonding & Ins. Co.

Dot Lemon Marriage Affidavit

The first marriage seemed to be a logical starting point. Who was this Brink, whom Dorothy, as then "Dorothy Culver Whitney," said she had married in 1927? Following this Brink thread revealed that one Leon Perl Brink (1895-1944) was a World War I pilot married not to Dorothy/Dot, but to another

14

woman, and he worked out of the Hayes Aviation Company in Cicero, New York in the late 1920s. Further searching showed that Brink had separated from his wife and family, and moved into a boarding house at 213 Green Street in Syracuse, New York , according to the 1930 Federal Census.[6] Brink's legal wife, Marian Riley Brink, was at that time living in the Nanticoke Township, Broome County, New York, according to the same 1930 census, with their daughter Norma Brink, born 13 December 1922. This Norma Brink surfaces in later research.

Much of this tangle of relationships was highly puzzling, given Dorothy's 1942 affidavit stating she had married Brink in 1927, and then Richmond Lemon in 1937. What was the origin of the connection between Dorothy and Brink, allegedly married in 1927? No official record of this marriage has been found. Further research curiously showed that Richmond "Doc" Lemon, whom Dot did in fact marry in 1937, had also been affiliated along with Leon Brink with Hayes Aviation in Cicero, New York in the late 1920s. So, total confusion, and still no early Dorothy (Dot Lemon) connection with Brink, prior to her 1942 affidavit alleging marriage to him in 1927.

More digging into the Hayes Aviation company in Cicero, New York, where both Leon Brink and William Richmond Lemon had been employed, revealed that one Dorothy Martin, in 1928, joined the staff of Hayes Aviation as a contract dealer. The same 1930 Census that showed Brink living in a boarding house at 213 Green Street in Syracuse New York, now astonishingly showed a Dorothy Martin,[7] living at the same address! Who was this Dorothy Martin? Once again the thought reoccurred: maybe she really was Jimmie Angel's estranged wife, Virginia Martin, with a changed first name. But, where did Dorothy Lemon, nee Brink fit into this melange of relationships, if at all?

1930 United States Federal Census

Name:	Leon P Brink
Birth Year:	1896
Gender:	Male
Race:	White
Age in 1930:	34
Birthplace:	New York
Marital Status:	Married
Relation to Head of House:	Lodger
Home in 1930:	Syracuse, Onondaga, New York, USA
Map of Home:	Syracuse, Onondaga, New York
Street Address:	Green
Ward of City:	6th
Block:	708
House Number:	213
Dwelling Number:	12
Family Number:	21
Age at First Marriage:	24
Attended School:	No
Able to Read and Write:	Yes
Father's Birthplace:	New York
Mother's Birthplace:	New York
Able to Speak English:	Yes
Occupation:	Aviator
Industry:	Aviation Co.
Class of Worker:	Wage or salary worker
Employment:	Yes
Veteran:	Yes
War:	WW

Household Members:	Name	Age
	Bert E Jones	57
	Elizabeth A Gaynor	52
	Jane S Chapman	52
	Charles Gauvere	50
	Carrie I Ruhl	50
	John C Quinterro	49
	Tecarus Brookman	47
	Margaret Brookman	39
	Leon P Brink	34
	Dorothy C Martin	22
	Frank Shapura	22
	Gerald A Beyea	22
	Lucylle Skapura	20

Source Citation: Year: *1930*; Census Place: *Syracuse, Onondaga, New York*;

1930 Census, Leon P. Brink

United States Census, 1930 for Dorothy C Martin

No image available

Name:	Dorothy C Martin
Event:	Census
Event Date:	1930
Event Place:	Syracuse, Onondaga, New York
Gender:	Female
Age:	22
Marital Status:	Single
Race:	White
Birthplace:	Wisconsin
Estimated Birth Year:	1908
Immigration Year:	
Relationship to Head of Household:	Lodger
Father's Birthplace:	Minnesota
Mother's Birthplace:	Illinois
Enumeration District Number:	0038
Family Number:	21
Sheet Number and Letter:	2B
Line Number:	75
NARA Publication:	T626, roll 1627
Film Number:	2341361
Digital Folder Number:	4639197
Image Number:	00264

Household	Gender	Age
Frank Shapura	M	22
Gerald A Beyea	M	22
Bert E Jones	M	57
John C Quinterro	M	49
Dorothy C Martin	F	22
Leon P Brink	M	34

1930 Census, Dorothy C. Martin

Was it possible this Dorothy Martin, working at Hayes Aviation, could later become Dorothy Brink, and then Dot Lemon? What about Dorothy Culver Whitney, the name Dorothy used in her affidavit in Miami in 1942? Incredible! I could scarcely imagine my dear semi-incapacitated Dot Lemon of Caracas as having been any of these people. Dorothy Brink, Dorothy Culver Whitney (whomever she may have been), wife of William Richmond Lemon, Virginia Angel nee Martin, or now a new Dorothy Martin, possibly connected to all of the above, or possibly to none of them. My research thus far had only seemed to complicate a story of myriad dimensions, not provide the answers I was seeking, in order to reveal a clear and traceable life history of my former Venezuelan charge, Dot Lemon. '

CHAPTER **4**

The Martin Family

THIS TANGLE OF marriages and alleged marriages raised more questions than it answered. As a next step, I looked further into the Dorothy Martin of the 1930 census. Now came to mind once again my earlier intuitive flash that Dot and Virginia Angel (nee Martin) could possibly have been the same person. I now had a Dorothy Martin with the same last name as Virginia Martin. So, who was Dorothy Martin, in apparent association with Leon Brink and Doc Lemon at Hayes Aviation, both of whom Dorothy Culver Whitney had listed as former (Brink) and current (Lemon) husbands? This had become a three- or even four-way, yet-to-be clarified mixture of identities and relationships.

Further research about this Dorothy Martin of the 1930 Census surfaced an Albert A. Martin,[8] who appears in the 1910 Census, as head of household, living in Lancaster, Nebraska. The dependents listed in this household included one Dorothy Martin, age 3, as an adopted daughter. The age of this adopted daughter in 1910, (3 years old), matched the age of the Dorothy Martin in the 1930 Census (age 23). Based on these records, my initial tentative conclusion, that the Dorothy Martin of Hayes Aviation was the adopted daughter of the 1910 census Albert A. Martin, was to be subsequently confirmed by Martin family descendants. So, the Dorothy Martin of the Hayes Aviation/ Brink/Lemon complex relationship was now to be revealed as the same Dorothy Martin (adopted) living in the same boarding house in Syracuse as Leon Brink in 1930.

Dot's complex life story, with the added complication of Dot as an adoptee, became for me an all-season quest never far from my daily thoughts. An earlier query to the Embassy in Caracas had been totally disappointing. The Embassy had failed to secure Dot's belongings, as required when a US Citizen dies

Dorothy Martin in household of Albert S Martin, "United States Census, 1910"

name:	**Dorothy Martin**
birthplace:	Wisconsin
relationship to head of household:	Adopted Daughter
residence:	Lancaster, Lancaster, Nebraska
marital status:	Single
race :	White
gender:	Female
immigration year:	
father's birthplace:	
mother's birthplace:	
family number:	311
page number:	14

	Household	Gender	Age	Birthplace
self	Albert S Martin	M	47y	Minnesota
wife	Clara D Martin	F	48y	Illinois
dau	Grace H Martin	F	22y	Wisconsin
son	Charles E Martin	M	20y	Wisconsin
dau	Aura B Martin	F	16y	Wisconsin
	Dorothy Martin	F	3y	Wisconsin

Citing this Record

"United States Census, 1910," index and images, *FamilySearch* (https://familysearch.org/pal:/MM9.1.1/ML42-R68 : accessed 24 Jan 2013), Dorothy Martin in household of Albert S Martin, Lancaster, Lancaster, Nebraska; citing sheet 14B, family 311, NARA microfilm publication T624, FHL microfilm 1374862.

The Church of Jesus Christ of Latter-day Saints | Church WebsitesClose Church Websites

1910 Census, Albert A. Martin

abroad without known relatives, and she had been buried in a pauper's grave site in Caracas.

Given that unproductive end I thus began to locate and contact descendants of Dorothy's adopted parents, Albert Alvin and Clara D. Martin. This was some five years into my efforts to plumb the life and circumstances of the Dot Lemon I had known in Venezuela.

Out-of-the-blue, now came one of several "eureka" research gems which appeared unexpectedly throughout my journey to understand and write the Dot Lemon story.

As a result of Martin intra-family communications[9] on my behalf, I was contacted by the daughter of Fern Marguerite Martin, granddaughter of Dorothy's adopted father, Albert A. Martin. What a milestone! This lady provided a trove of photos and other Dot Lemon (then Dorothy Martin) material. At the time I considered this the mother lode of historical material about Dot Lemon, but there were yet later revelations.

The note to me from Albert Martin's great granddaughter said, "The following history with accompanying anecdotes was handwritten as remembered by Fern Marguerite Martin."

It was typed(unedited) by Fern's own daughter Mary Carmella.

In the early 1920s the Martin family moved from Nebraska to Central New York, where after failing at farming, Rev. Martin became pastor of the Breakabeen Presbyterian Church in Breakabeen, New York. Dorothy attended Middleburg High School in central New York State from about 1923-25.

My grandfather Martin had been an evangelistic minister in Milwaukee before moving to Nebraska. He had also worked in an orphanage there. He found twins a boy and a girl - on the steps of the orphanage in a clothes

Dorothy Martin c. 1925

basket. The baby boy died but the girl was adopted by my grandparents. Dorothy wasn't treated very well by the Martins.

They never let her forget she was adopted. In the morning, before school she milked three cows, ate breakfast and changed clothes. After school she did the day's dishes, again milked cows, then did homework.

I guess from all accounts she was rather incorrigible! She could dance, learned the Charleston and taught Lucille [Dorothy's step-sister]to do it ... and she played the piano very well.

Not surprisingly, probably chafing at a difficult farm life and a religious father, Dorothy left home at the age of 18 (1925) to live in Syracuse with a cousin, Laurence Ellsworth, from her foster mother's side of the Martin family.

By 1930 she was living in the same boarding house as Leon Brink in Syracuse.

Given this description of a difficult, somewhat abused life as an adopted child, and the description of Dot by her sibling and author of the handwritten letter as lively, "incorrigible," musical and fun-loving, it is not difficult to imagine Dorothy as anxious to escape the Martin family and begin her own life. Reference in the Martin family notes to twin foundlings validated Dot's account of a twin brother, relayed often to my wife and me at dinner those many years ago in Caracas in 1972. Dot never revealed to me in Venezuela that she had been adopted, nor much less revealed her beginning as a foundling. Further details seemed to me, at this stage of my research, to be most certainly unavailable and unknowable.

The historical record of Dot's life in the early 1920s, when it seems she attended the Bush School of Music in Chicago, and from the early 1930s before arriving in Florida about 1935, has been challenging and obscure. These periods in her life will be treated more extensively later in the story. Until now, my efforts to know Dorothy's life story as a Martin uncovered an early adoption, prior to 1910, when she was a member of the Albert S. Martin household in Wisconsin. What followed in her life story composed of marriages and a career as a pilot and other ventures, grew ever more complicated.

CHAPTER 5

Taking Off ... A New Flying Life

IN 1926, BEFORE any marriages would have taken place, Dorothy nee Martin, adopted daughter of the Presbyterian minister, had now left home and was located in Rochester, New York, where she appears in the Rochester City Directory showing employment as a nurse and maid. In later documents Dot also alludes to or lists university courses taken around this time, which offer possibilities as to how she acquired some of her later acknowledged skills in both music and navigation. It is in Rochester where we pick up on the next and formative phase of Dorothy's life, in which she is fascinated with flight and becomes a pilot.

Following is an excerpt from an article discovered in the Rochester, NY press (date unknown) by Kenneth Stratton,[10] presumably written some years later, circa 1940, perhaps after the author, Stratton, had become aware of Dorothy's barnstorming and flying activity at Hayes Aviation near Rochester.

> "One afternoon early in 1926 Dorothy and I, both aspiring young law students, went out to 'The Flying Field' where the city of Rochester (NY) is now located. We had

heard that there was an airplane there, and we both took rides. When we got back on the ground again, the pilot asked us why didn't we learn to fly. I turned to Dot. She stood staring at the Jenny, her eyes glistening. Turning to me she whispered in an awed voice, 'Kenny, do you really think we could learn?' From that day Dorothy lived aviation."

This article goes on to say

"The little spare time she had was spent in studying meteorology and navigation with an eminent authority (identity unknown) on these subjects, at that time teaching in Syracuse. From this eminent authority Dot learned to use a sextant and from there, to plot a velocity vector. Today, she is considered by experts to be one of the best informed pilots on meteorology and air mass analysis."

This reference to Dorothy's technical studies offers a plausible background to her later success at the Institute of Navigation.

Subsequent online research of Government records uncovered the beginning point of her professional life as a pilot. In an application for a pilot's license filed with the Department of Commerce, Dade County, Florida on 1 June 1937,[11] and signed Dorothy Lemon, she affirmed flight instruction May-December 1926 by Major Merrill K. Riddick, at the Rochester Municipal Airport. Dorothy later added that she had soloed in a Jenny/ Canuck single engine aircraft on 1 May 1926, her instructor being Captain Merrill K. Riddick, who was a WWI pilot of considerable renown. Dorothy included the information detailing her first solo flight in her bio sketch from the Archives of the International Woman's Air and Space Museum (IWASM),

Cleveland, Ohio. In this same pilot license application Dorothy also listed under Education, "Conservatory of Music, Chicago and Albany Law school." Dorothy's flight instructor, this afore-mentioned Major Merrill K. Riddick, had an impressive history.

Pilot License Application, 1937

147

13. Experience as pilot, that is, as the sole operator of the controls and in command of aircraft in flight..........
    (a) Name flying fields where you received instructions and their locations..........
        Belevedere Airport West Palm Beach Fla.
        Rochester Municipal Airport Rochester New York
    (b) Name instructors and give dates..Major Merrill K. Riddick-May-Dec. 1926.
    W.R. Lemon Aug.1935.
                                                  265:30
    (c) Solo hours in last 60 days..84:3a Solo hours in last year 265:30 Total solo hours 270:30
    (d) Name fields where you have operated; give dates and names of employers..........
    Belvedere Airport..1936
    Morrison Field....1937

    (e) Are you applying as a graduate of an Approved School?..No
    Name of Approved School..........
    Course from which graduated (Tran., LC., Pri., Solo)..........
    Is certificate of graduation attached?..........
    Total dual hours.......... Total solo hours..........
    (f) Name types flown and hours in each..........
    Stinson - 12 hours
    Bird - 55 hours
    Taylor Cub Kinner - 2 hours
        201:30 hours

14. Experience and training on aircraft engines, giving types with which familiar and length of experience on each
    Wright J-5   Assisted in both major and top overhauls on types
    Kinner K-5   mentioned . Have taken care of and maintained
    CK5   service on Kinner for 1 year, and Continental for
    Continental A-40   6 months

15. Experience as to airplane structure and rigging, giving types with which familiar and length of experience on each........Familiar with rigging on Kinner Bird

16. Have you read the Air Commerce Regulations?..Yes
17. AFFIDAVIT:
    State....FLORIDA
    County....DADE   ss.
    I hereby swear that the statements contained in this application are true.

    Dated this....1st....day of....JUNE...., 1937

                                     Dorothy Lemon
                                     (Signature)

    Subscribed and sworn to before me this....1....day of....June...., 1937
                                  Eleanor N. Shields
                                     Notary Public.

My commission expires..........., 19....

DIRECTIONS

1. Application for only one class of license may be made on this form.
2. The physical examination must be taken before an authorized medical examiner of the Department of Commerce. In case applicant is a regular or reserve pilot of the Army, Navy or Marine Corps, he may instead submit a copy of an Army or Navy physical examination for flying, if such examination has been made within the last six (6) months. Certificate of the result of such examination will not be accepted.
3. The applicant must furnish a licensed aircraft for the tests involved.

                                                  133 C
U. S. GOVERNMENT PRINTING OFFICE 1932   11—9724

Pilot License Application, 1937 (pg.2)

MERRILL K. (Hobo of the Air) RIDDICK 1895-1988.

One of many amazing aspects of Dot's life story were her encounters with a number of famous, infamous, and well known public figures, some of whom will appear later in this story. Riddick, the first, was a politician and aviator, who actually campaigned for President of the United States three times as the candidate of the "Puritan Ethic and Epic, Magnetohydrodynamics and Prohibition Party," in 1976, 1980 and 1984. His father was Carl Wood Riddick, US Congressman from Montana 1919-1923.

In 1917, Merrill K. Riddick was a member of the first graduating class from the Army Air Force Aeronautics School in San Diego, California. During World War I he flew with the US Army in Europe. Returned from the war, Riddick was among the first airmail pilots, after which Riddick and Charles A. Lindbergh barnstormed together and flew in the Harry Perkins Air Circus. From 1926-28 Riddick was an instructor at the first aviation preparatory school in Rochester, New York. This was Dorothy's exotic flight instructor, a man who once landed his plane on a residential street in defiance of the police near his father's house in Washington, DC. He flew away when he was good and ready! There seems little doubt that this character influenced Dorothy's next adventure, and her subsequent interest in flying, navigation, astrology, and meteorology, subjects which in large part defined the rest of Dorothy's life.

Barnstorming

As noted earlier, barnstormers were itinerant pilots who toured the country, offering plane rides wherever they could find paying customers, usually in rural small towns. That the adventurous life of a barnstormer should appeal and become the next phase of Dorothy's life seemed to me a natural progression of her recent departure from the confines of the Martin family, and newly discovered fascination with flying. The following is an excerpt (pages 179-181) from the book "Women With Wings" by Charles E. Planck in 1942.[13]

She learned to fly in 1926 in Rochester, N.Y., where she worked with such ardor in the promotion of a flying club that she was soon managing the Rochester airport itself. After a year or so of this, she went "on tour," the only girl with four young barnstorming pilots in the Spring of 1928. A Georgia tornado destroyed their planes and ended the "tour." After the barnstorming debacle in Georgia, Dorothy returned north and in 1928 joined the staff of a new firm, The Hayes Aviation Company, as a contract dealer. Six months later, representing the "American Eagle" agency she was made salesman for the upper territory of New York, western Pennsylvania and western Vermont. By 1930 she had copped the record for all sales east of the Mississippi for having sold in three months fourteen airplanes, all costing above $5000. While working at Hayes Aviation, what little spare time she had was spent in studying meteorology and navigation with an eminent authority (NFI) on these subjects, then teaching in Syracuse. From him she learned to use a sextant and plot a velocity vector. She began and still continues the study of weather. Today, she is considered by experts to be one of the best informed pilots on meteorology and air mass analysis.

(Much of this same information was included in the Kenneth Stratton newspaper article cited above. The book "Women With Wings" was published in 1942, and the author does not cite sources for the Dot Lemon information included in his book. The Stratton article appeared circa 1940, written as though Dorothy and Stratton were in Rochester together when both had

Lady Mary Heath, British Aviatrix, Flies to Cicero

Lady Mary Heath, famous English aviatrix, will land her plane this afternoon at the Hayes airport in Cicero, and be the guest of honor at a tea given by Miss Dorothy Martin, saleswoman for the company, who is a close friend of the titled English woman.

Lady Heath will make the Hayes airport her headquarters while she is in Syracuse.

She flew from Cortland to Cazenovia Sunday, escorted by Miss Martin and Leon Brink, chief pilot for Hayes Aviation Company, Inc.

their first plane ride, in 1926. It would thus appear that author Planck received his book information about Dot Lemon either from the Stratton newspaper article or from Stratton himself.)

On 23 July 1929, the Syracuse Herald newspaper published an item noting "Lady Mary Heath, (also known as Lady Icarus) famous English aviatrix, will land her plane this afternoon at the Hayes Airport in Cicero, and be the guest of honor at a tea given by Miss Dorothy Martin, who is a close friend of the titled English woman." The article noted that Lady Heath had been escorted by Miss Martin and Leon Brink, chief pilot for Hayes Aviation Company, while flying from Cortland to Casanova (New York).[12]

Here some dates conflict with Dorothy's later 1942 statement of having married Brink in 1927. In this 1929 article Dorothy is still Miss Martin. Further to Dorothy's late 1920s short-lived barnstorming adventure, it seems probable that two of her male pilot comrades at that time may have been the Enslow brothers, Wilder and Randy, both of whom had subsequent flying careers. Wilder was a WWI flyer and one of the first million-mile airline pilot captains. In 1945 in Savannah, Georgia Capt. Wilder Enslow was named head of a newly formed organization, the "Air Legion of the American Air Veterans Organization" a club of veteran airmen from WWI and II, as well as Civil Air Patrol (CAP) members and other war veteran pilots. Members were to be equipped with uniforms

A Pencil Sketch Of A Pilot

By Kenneth Stratton

While visiting in Florida, I heard that the subject of this article had been asked for a story about herself. I sought permission to write it, and consider it a privilege if I may give a brief sketch of Dot Lemon who, with great singleness of purpose, and without thought of reward, has turned her efforts for the past fifteen years to the progress of aviation.

One afternoon, early in 1926, Dot and I, both aspiring young law students, went out to "The Flying Field" where Rochester (N. Y.) airport is now. We had heard there was an airplane, out there. We both took rides. When we got back on the ground again, the pilot asked us why we didn't learn to fly. I turned to Dot. She stood staring at the Jenny, her eyes glistening. Turning to me, she whispered in an awed voice, "Kenny, do you really think we could learn?"

From that day Dot lived aviation.

From The Bottom Up

Many people embark upon a career to gain wealth and social position. Dot gave up wealth and social position to embark upon a career. With her insatiable curiosity she took motors down and put them back together. She did the hard and grimy work on them that was necessary for the overhauls, cleaning carbon from the parts and grinding valves until she learned to fit piston rings, and time the valves and magnetos. She studied the fundamentals of metallurgy. She learned to weld and to use a micrometer and a pair of calipers. She studied electricity. When it came time to put an airplane together, she was right there, stitching, and doping and learning to rig the wings.

The next year she went barnstorming and experienced all the tribulations of her contemporaries.

In 1929 she was employed by the firm of Hayes Aviation in Syracuse, N. Y. They put her in the Sales Department, and I have good authority that there are still people today who say they bought an airplane from her, who had no intention of buying anything from anybody. The little spare time she had was spent in studying meteorology and navigation with an eminent authority on these subjects, then teaching in Syracuse. From him she learned to use a sextant and plot a velocity vector. She began and still continues the study of weather. Today, she is considered by experts to be one of the best informed pilots on meteorology and air mass analysis.

Some 14 years ago, in a little town in Georgia, four men and a girl, all young barnstorming pilots, sat in a hotel room one night. That day a tornado had ripped across the little town, twisting their airplanes into grotesque shapes. They had no money and had not eaten all day. The men all swore if they ever got home they would never go near an airplane again. The girl started talking.

For two hours these four young gentlemen were treated to oratory such as they were not to hear again for many a long day. Eloquently she reproached them for quitting. She painted a vivid picture of aviation and its future place in the world. She paced up and down the room, her words darting and thrusting at each one

Dot Lemon

like small swords. Then she began to cheer, and her words inspired new confidence in those who had so lately been discouraged.

As they went down the hall to their rooms, each was busy thinking how he could get another airplane. It did not matter that they had not eaten for 24 hours and were a thousand miles from home. Today two of those men have comfortable berths in the field of flying. The other two are leading figures in American aviation. The girl was Dot Lemon.

Today, she and her husband, Dick Lemon, run a flying school in West Palm Beach, Fla. At Christmas time the cards and messages of good will come by the

(See FEMININE PILOT, page 41)

31

and special gold wing insignia.

Dorothy's aborted barnstorming adventure in Georgia, and her record at Hayes Aviation, have been documented in books and news articles. Her barnstorming companions' names are speculative (the Enslow brothers) but the possible accuracy is buttressed by the listing in her Contemporary Authors biography of membership in the "Air Legion of American Air Veterans Organization" where Wilder S. Enslow headed a Georgia/S. Carolina/Florida District of the Legion.[14]

According to an 8 January 1948 article[15] in the Oklahoma City Times, "Dot received a gold metal emblem pin of the Veteran Pilot's Association. The pin is gold and has a winged world with three diamonds surrounded by the Roman Numerals of a clock, depicting time." The newspaper article goes on to say, "Mrs. Lemon is the only woman in the world who has won this award." Dot highly treasured the pin and in a personal letter to unnamed friends, described how she always had it secured by a safety pin. It was subsequently stolen from her hotel room in Venezuela. I believe this medal indeed came from the organization formed in 1945 in Georgia called the "Air Legion of the American Air Veterans Organization." The aforementioned Capt. Wilder Enslow was the regional Director of the Legion, and it is likely, in my mind, that he was acquainted with Dot (then Dorothy Martin) during her late 1920s barnstorming adventures.

Dot's reputation as one of the leading navigation experts for that era seems to have been well accepted, but documenting her formal education in navigation and other university studies has been difficult, despite her claims to have attended various institutions. Her navigation knowledge and skills provided the basis for her later leadership of the professional organization, the Institute of Navigation (ION), something which reveals her exceptional intelligence and amazing abilities among women with wings of that era.

CITY AVIATRIX GETS GLOBAL AWARD

Don't let her fool you. That "It doesn't mean anything" pose is a fake. She's really so thrilled, she's been leaving sparkling trails of excitement in her wake.

Dot Lemon's friends could only smile indulgently as she incoherently twittered something about "veteran pilot pin . . . took 25 years . . . I finally made it . . . golly, I'm so excited!"

Oklahoma City's famed aviatrix has finally achieved her heart's desire. This week she received the Veteran Pilot's emblem from the Veteran Pilots association, of which she is a member.

Mrs. Lemon, who has been living at 217½ Harrison, is the only woman in the world who has won this award.

In fact, only about 12 fliers have received the emblem—all of them men.

The pin is gold and has a winged world with three diamonds, surrounded by the Roman numerals of a clock, depicting time.

"And time is what it took, too," the copper-haired flier mused. "I've been flying 25 years, and have about 11,300 hours to my credit. That took time!"

From the time she began her flying career in an old "Jenny" back in New York state, Dot Lemon has steadily and spectacularly moved to the top ranks of aviation. Her favorite plane is the one in which patrons at Downtown airport have seen her zooming around, a silver AT-6 dubbed "Cookie Dough."

Mrs. Lemon, wife of Dick Lemon, Houston, Texas, also a well-known pilot, has flown all over the United States, Central and South America, Mexico, the West Indies and Cuba.

Among the long list of aviation positions she has held are those of chief pilot and instructor for the Airline Instrument unit; fixed base operator for 13 years at West Palm Beach, Fla.; pilot for Associated Press photographers in Florida; flight commander and instructor on an army program in Tulsa and a member of a 9-member civilian consulting board on a service instrument flight program during the war.

Mrs. Lemon is widely known as an authority on instrument flying.

Now she has a new star to paste by her name . . . that of executive. She will assume duties January 4 with a major oil company, with headquarters in New York.

Dot will take over as head of the company's newly-formed aviation division.

City Aviatrix Gets Global Award

The energetic and attractive Mrs. Lemon is, at 44, the only woman to wear the diamond-studded wings of a senior pilot, earned only with 10,000 logged hours. She has approximately 12,500 hours to her credit now, much of it night and bad weather flying on instruments.

Most noted for her work in the development and teaching of instrument flying, she has also written a book on meteorology. She ranked high in civilian air work for the army during the war, and won a government award for bad weather observation flying. Since the war she has been made head of the aviation department of Petroleum Industries of New York and Houston.

A close second in the Kendall Trophy race at Cleveland last year was the latest in a long list of races in which she has never failed to finish in the money.

Dot and her husband, who is also in the aviation industry, recently moved to Houston, choosing this city both for their home and for this major speedrun because, they explain, they found here the most vigorous interest in aviation of any city in the nation. It is a city rapidly growing in importance as an International Air Gateway.

Last year Houston entered more planes in the Cleveland races than any other city, taking under the colors of Glenn McCarthy, three of the four top places in the Bendix race.

Mrs. Lemon says she feels that flying events of international importance should become a regular feature in Texas.

Veteran Pilot Pin Award

CHAPTER 6

Marriage and Family

THE QUESTION OF Dot's marriage(s) and children is very complicated and a major enigma in Dot's life story. In 1942 the affidavit signed Dorothy Lemon affirmed her earlier marriage (1927) and subsequent divorce from Leon Brink, as well as her marriage to Dick Lemon in 1937. As we know, both Brink and Lemon were affiliated with Hayes Aviation in Cicero, NY, where Dorothy landed work after her ill-fated barnstorming adventure in Georgia in the Spring of 1928. Dorothy's 1942 affidavit says she married Brink in 1927, but according to the 1930 Federal census, she is listed as Dorothy Martin, living in Syracuse in the same boarding house as Brink, who was married, but not living with his wife. I have found no record of Dorothy's alleged marriage to Brink in Rochester in 1927, and the certificate of the Brink divorce from his actual wife (Marian Riley Brink) was dated some years later. While Dorothy's relationship with Brink in the 1927-1930 time frame is open to speculation, Dorothy, still Martin, is listed in the Syracuse City Directory in 1930 and 1931.

Jumping forward in time, Lemon children are mentioned, but this aspect of Dorothy's life remains the most difficult to piece together. In an interview published some thirty years later, in the San Diego Evening Tribune 16 June 1962, Dot says after leaving Hayes Aviation, she arrived in Florida with her four children (date unknown) where she began flying passengers up and down the beach for $2.50 a ride.

There seems to be a major gap here in time lines as well as explanations regarding the parentage of the four boys, where and when they were born, and finally, the date that Dot actually arrived in Florida. Dot never claimed William Richmond Lemon to be the father of her boys; she actually only attributed them to her "first husband," but did not mention this first husband's name. Although a marriage to Brink seems improbable due to lack of documentation and his status as a married man whose legal spouse was Marian Riley Brink, he is the only known candidate as father of Dot's claimed four boys, whose actual existence also remains an open question. These unanswered and unexplained issues, especially regarding the boys, were a continuing dilemma throughout my years of research. By 1936, Mrs. Dorothy C. Brink is listed as Sec-Treas, Flying Service of the W.R. Lemon Inc. flying service at Belvedere Airport, West Palm Beach, Florida.[16]

I thus located her in Florida at this date, still identifying herself as Dorothy Culver Brink. It is here in Florida where her four boys, named William, Clinton, Wellington, and Sherwood should appear if born in the 1930-35 time frame, as seems logical. Two first-person sources have offered conflicting information. Dick Stine, who worked at Belvedere airport in Florida and took flying lessons from Dorothy about 1937, related the following story. He said he had traded an old Cushman motorcycle for flying lessons from Dorothy. Eventually he made his initial solo flight from West Palm Beach to Miami, having never previously gotten out of the landing pattern, doing only take-offs and landings with Dorothy. Stine stated he had never seen any children of Dorothy at the airport, and none were ever mentioned.

However, an unidentified source, a pilot, allegedly told of having seen four little boys racing about at that same airport. In 2010, further research identified a grandson of Leon Brink, who

Florida Profit

W.R. LEMON INCORPORATED

PRINCIPAL ADDRESS
BELVEDERE AIRPORT
WEST PALM BEACH FL

MAILING ADDRESS
BELVEDERE AIRPORT
WEST PALM BEACH FL

Document Number	FEI Number	Date Filed
132884	000000000	08/18/1936
State	**Status**	**Effective Date**
FL	INACTIVE	NONE
Last Event	**Event Date Filed**	**Event Effective Date**
DISSOLVED BY PROCLAMATION	09/02/1941	NONE

Registered Agent

Name & Address
LEMON, W.R. BELVEDERE AIRPORT WEST PALM BCH. FL

Officer/Director Detail

Name & Address	Title
LEMON, W.R. BELVEDERE AIRPORT W.PALM BCH. FL	PD
O'CONNELL., PHIL 613 HARVEY BLDG. W.PALM BCH. FL	VD
BRINK, DOROTHY C. BELVEDERE AIRPORT	STD

W.R. Lemon Inc.

said in a phone interview he remembered his grandmother (Leon Brink's legal wife) referring to the four boys and mentioning the names "Big Red" and "Sherwood," and that he was sure Leon Brink was the father of the boys. When I subsequently visited this grandson at his home in New York State he nervously recanted, saying he had been confused. During this same visit I spoke at length with another grandson, who said his grandmother's diaries had never mentioned these alleged boys, and he did not believe in their existence as possible sons of Leon Brink.

Dorothy's actual whereabouts from 1932-35 remain unsubstantiated, although she later claimed she had been in Florida during this period. According to her Florida marriage license she married Dick Lemon on 3 April 1937, whom she would have met in New York at Hayes Aviation in 1928-30, but perhaps only later joined in Florida. This seems a probable way of organising the chronology of her married life.

The Boys ... Fact or Fiction?

As Dot's promising accomplishments began to take shape in those early years, soon thereafter so did her story as a mother. There are several conflicting explanations as to whether Dot's sons were real or whether they were a product of her fertile imagination. If William, Clinton, Sherwood, and Wellington actually existed, they were most likely born between 1931 and 1935, when Dorothy's location is not certain. The fact or fiction of the existence of her claimed four sons remains perplexing and quite exasperating. Numerous press articles about Dorothy Lemon the pilot, written by admiring local newspapers during the 40s and 50s, referred to Dorothy as the mother of four boys. The boys appear by first name in official State Department[17] documents; furthermore, she referred to them more than once in correspondence.[18]

In a letter[19] postmarked 5 April 1964 written to a close friend, Dot writes,

"The anguished day of 22 March 1964, when one of my flesh to whom I had given birth, and another loved one, whose name I carry, were lying still and without breath. Each of us far away from the other as preparations progressed to seal away their bodies. This day, Frenzy thrust itself into the brain and in turn had to be thrust back out. This Day no speech would come. Only walking and walking and walking. This handwringing Day, when a keening cry would force itself unwanted and unexpectedly from a stunned throat. This Day your flowers made double efforts to send out their cry, and again and again and still again. Gradually quiet came to comfort a ripped and flagellated heart. If I had not had your words to read, your flowers to speak, as only flowers can speak, I wonder if that Day would ever ever have come to an end.

"For these words of yours, for the flowers, and for your own dear selves, I send you my deepest gratitude and love."

Dot in this letter is referring to son Clinton (killed in a car accident earlier in March), and husband "Doc" Lemon who died 20 March 1964, that same year, in Sullivan, Missouri. She ends this letter saying, "Sherwood and his family and Wellington wish me to tell you they appreciate how much you did for me."

Could such heartfelt pain and agony have poured forth from other than a truly anguished mother in remembrance of other than her own flesh and blood son, and husband? In citing messages fron sons Sherwood and Wellington in this letter, it seems more than likely that Sherwood and Wellington would have been personally known to the recipients of the letter, and that the boys were real persons.

Here I found it difficult to imagine that Dot did not truly, in her own mind, believe in the existence of her sons. It could follow that in referring to sons in her written letters she was logically, to her, reinforcing such a belief. I believe it also possible that the four sons were part of a fantasy, such as that which is created by very imaginative people; for example she also claimed to be a member of Danish royalty.

```
UNCLASSIFIED

PAGE 01          CARACA  07492  051650Z         RELEASED IN PART
ACTION OCS-06                                    B6

INFO  LOG-00   ADS-00   H-01    AMAD-01  /008 W
                        ------------------217675  051935Z /38
R 051649Z AUG 86
FM AMEMBASSY CARACAS
TO SECSTATE WASHDC 2872

UNCLAS CARACAS 07492

E.O. 12356: N/A
TAGS: CASC (LEMON, DOT CULVER WHITNEY)
SUBJECT: DEATH OF US CITIZEN DOT C. W. LEMON

REF: A.CARACAS 7068, B.STATE 233638, C.MUNICH 3071

1.  FUNERAL SERVICES FOR DOT LEMON WERE HELD AT THE DIAZ
FUNERAL HOME ON 23 JULY 1986.  BURIAL WAS IN CEMENTERIO
MARAURY, LA GUAIRITA, ZONE 5, SECTION 304, QUADRANT I,
MODULE "C".

2.  ALL ARRANGEMENTS AND PAYMENT FOR SERVICES WERE MADE
BY SR. IVAN GOMEZ WITHOUT CONCURRENCE OF POST.  SR.
GOMEZ HELD POWER OF ATTORNEY FOR MRS. LEMON.  UNDER
VENEZUELAN LAW, POA BECAME INEFFECTIVE WHEN MRS. LEMON
DIED.

3.  CONOFF COLLECTED NINE CONTAINERS OF EFFECTS FROM
APARTMENT OF MRS. LEMON LOCATED IN LOS PALOS GRANDES,
CARACAS, EDIFICIO PASCAL, NO. 73-B, 7TH FLOOR.  EFFECTS
HAVE BEEN STORED SECURELY IN THE EMBASSY WAREHOUSE.
VALUE OF ITEMS IS NEGLIGIBLE.

4.  THROUGH DOCUMENTS AND INTERVIEWS, POST DISCOVERED
THAT DOT LEMON HAD FOUR SONS: WILLIAM, SHERWOOD, CLINTON
AND WELLINGTON. OTHER FAMILY SURVIVORS MAY INCLUDE:

UNCLASSIFIED

UNCLASSIFIED

PAGE 02        CARACA  07492  051650Z

-      CHARLES LEMON, [            ] (REF. A & C)
-      JAMES OZBUN, [
-                   ]
-      BLANCHE LEMON, [          ]
```

PPT service
1-877 487 7778

UNITED STATES DEPARTMENT OF STATE
REVIEW AUTHORITY: ROBERT R STRAND
DATE/CASE ID: 25 AUG 2006 200602703   UNCLASSIFIED

CHAPTER 7

Childhood According to Dorothy

ON 5 DECEMBER 1936, in West Palm Beach, Florida, Dorothy applied for U.S. Social Security. Her official application[20] shows her name as Dorothy Whitney Brink, the date and place of birth as August 22, 1907, in Chicago, Illinois. The official application is signed Dorothy C. Brink. But now, some new names appear, this time in reference to her lineage! This application gives her [birth] father's name as Albert Arlington Whitney, and her mother's name as Dorothy Ellsworth Hubbell. Note: Albert is the first name of her adopted father, A.A. Martin; Ellsworth is the maiden name of her adopted mother, Clara Ellsworth Martin. This is the moment in time when Dorothy first claims that she is a member of the heretofore unmentioned Whitney family.

Five years later, additional Whitney family documentation comes to light. On January 6, 1942, in Miami, Florida, Dorothy C. Lemon filed a sworn statement[22] certifying a true copy of her original Certificate of Birth[21] No. 97682.20. This birth certificate states that Dorothy Culver Whitney was born August 22, 1907, in Cook County, Illinois. Dorothy's father is listed as Albert Arlington Whitney, resident at 1000 Lake Shore Drive, Chicago, age thirty-four at time of Dorothy's birth. Her father's

Form SS-5 TREASURY DEPARTMENT INTERNAL REVENUE SERVICE	U. S. SOCIAL SECURITY ACT APPLICATION FOR ACCOUNT NUMBER 263-05-7463	

Lemon Social Security Application

birthplace is shown as Boston, Massachusetts; his occupation is listed as "Minister of the Gospel." Dorothy's mother is shown as Dorothy Catherine Hubbell, residing at the same Lake Shore Drive address, and born in Wheaton, Illinois. Her occupation is listed as house wife. Age at time of Dorothy's birth, thirty. This certificate of birth shows an Attending Physician Certification that confirms her date of birth as August 22 , 1907; but this important document was filed 34 years later, on November 18, 1941, and only certified by Dot herself.

Once again, things became ever more complicated and interesting. Up to this moment, I had known that Dorothy was the adopted daughter of Albert Alvin Martin, her birth place and natural parentage unknown. According to the 1910 and 1920 Federal Census, the Martin family, including Dorothy, resided in Omaha, Nebraska. However, in 1936 (date of her own Social Security application), Dorothy first mentions her alleged Whitney family parentage, and in her 1942 certified (by her) birth certificate, shows her birthplace as Chicago, residence 1000 /1020 Lake Shore Drive. Her Social Security application and her newly minted birth certificate both show her Whitney

Dot Lemon Birth Certificate

53

MIAMI, FLORIDA
6 JANUARY 1942

I CERTIFY THIS THIS IS A TRUE COPY OF THE
ORIGINAL OF CERTIFICATE OF BIRTH No. 97682.

Dorothy C. Lemon

SUBSCRIBED AND SWORN TO BEFORE ME AT MIAMI,
FLORIDA, THIS 6TH DAY OF JANUARY 1942.

Elizabeth Davis

Notary Public, State of Florida at large.
My commission expires Dec. 2, 1945.
Bonded by Mass Bonding & Ins. Co

48a

Lemon Birth Certificate Affidavit

44

father as being of the same profession, religious clergy, and having the same first name as her adopted Martin father! While the Martin family had been documented, Dot's newly acquired Whitney parentage remained obscure, perhaps even conjured up in Dot's alternate life mosaic, with the identity of her birth father as yet unverified excepting this reissued birth certificate.

At this point in my efforts to untangle Dot's life, I was frustrated and confused at seemingly inexplicable and perhaps contradictory dates and places. If Dot was truly a foundling, under what circumstance could the Whitney family have actually given her up for adoption? This birth certificate was a copy; originals were destroyed in an earlier Cook County, Chicago fire. Was there a birth father named Whitney, as yet to be identified and confirmed? Without forthcoming answers, I remained beset by the many conflicting parts of Dot's life yet to be sorted out, but found I could not give up. I maintained hope that future clarifications might emerge as to Dot's true birth identity and facts of life.

My next discovery came in the form of a bio-bibliographic guide to current authors published by Gale Research Company, 2200 Book Tower, Detroit 26, Michigan, entitled Contemporary Authors.[23] This came courtesy of the International Women's Air and Space Museum (IWASM) in Cleveland, Ohio, and contains a rather complete record of Dot Lemon's life, probably written in the early 1960s following publication of her book "One-One" in 1963.

The extensive and exclusive information contained in the curriculum vitae, however, almost certainly came from Dot herself and so is considered as her version, as valid as that might be. According to this Contemporary Authors document, her name was Dot Whitney Lemon, her date of birth August 22, 1906 (not 1907 as stated in her Social Security application), and birth place in Chicago, Illinois. Her father's name is Albert Arlington Whitney; her mother's name (of Danish lineage) is shown as Dorothy Katherine-Skane-Holland-Rosenkrans-Carlsen-Christiansen-Requa-Hubbell. This elaborates considerably on her alleged birth certificate, which shows her mother as Dorothy Catherine Hubbell, as well as throwing in possible Danish names, a heritage which I now remembered she had claimed in conversations with my wife and me in Caracas. Her husband is listed as William Richmond Lemon, (this would be Doc Lemon) date of marriage April 4, 1929.

The actual date of marriage to Lemon is April 4, 1937. Spouse vocation is listed as "Invalid." (In other correspondence circa late 1950s Dot referred to her husband as a drunk; thus most likely, the description of him as an "invalid.") Doc Lemon died in 1964 in Missouri. Children by (her) 1st marriage, presumably Brink, are listed as William, Sherwood, Clinton, and Wellington, and there are no children by second marriage. Her current address was given as 1840 Camino Palmero, Hollywood, California.

As I've mentioned, there is no record of a first marriage; the identity of four sons has not been documented, nor has their actual existence been verified. Her childhood, however, is given in some detail, as written in Contemporary Authors:

> "She was educated by private tutor and music teachers starting at the age of 4. Had 4 years of public school and 5 years at Bush Conservatory of Music,[24] Chicago, Illinois. In 1921 at 15 years old Mrs. Lemon had a high school diploma. In 3 years she had done the work of the regular 4 year course with 6 subjects in each semester. 4 years each of Latin, French, Mathematics, English, History, Biology 2 yrs., Civics 2 years. At the age of 15 Mrs. Lemon had passed the entrance exams of 4 universities and 3 colleges but was considered by her family too young to enter any of these Institutions."

Bush Conservatory of Music

In November of 1936 Dorothy filed an "Application for Pilot's License" with the Department of Commerce, Aeronautics Branch.[25] It appears her flying prior to 1936 was done on a student license, not uncommon in that era of early aviation. In this application Dorothy is more specific regarding her post-high school experience. She noted her education as "Private Tutor, Grade School, Chicago Conservatory of Music (Graduate), Albany Law School (Graduate), one year P.G. Columbia University, 3-month course Harmony and Orchestration, Eastman School of Music, Rochester New York." The Albany Law school is mentioned in the earlier Kenneth Stratton article, which noted her introduction to flying at Rochester, New York in 1926. Other school attendance cited by Dorothy has not been verified, although her piano skills during high school were cited in notes from a descendant of her adopted Martin family.

Quite a record!! ... and much more. With this information Dorothy had constructed an outline of her early childhood, that included not only her alleged Whitney parentage, first surfaced by her in 1936, but also her residence at 1000/1020 Lake Shore Drive, Chicago. Dot would have been about fifty-six years of age if this bio was written in 1963. In this version of her history she has now omitted her previous claimed marriage to Leon

Form AB-19
Revised 4-1-33

DEPARTMENT OF COMMERCE
AERONAUTICS BRANCH

APPLICATION FOR PILOT'S LICENSE

To the Secretary of Commerce:

APPLICATION NO.
91029

LICENSE NO.
36251

RECOMMENDED FOR

Private

WAS L.A. ISSUED

yes

NAME BASE IF FOR LIMITED COMMERCIAL

DATE

NOV. 10-1936

INSPECTOR

Application is hereby made for a ...LIMITED..COMMERCIAL... LICENSE
(Transport—limited commercial—private—solo—glider)

1. Name Dorothy..Ø.........WHITNEY....Brink...........
   (Print or type)   (First name)   (Middle name)   (Surname)

2. Permanent address 1527..I..St..............Box151..Lake..Worth...
   (Street)   (Post Office)

   ..Florida..............Palm..Beach.........9139......
   (State)   (County)   (Telephone)

   NOTE.—Applicant must advise of any change of address.

3. Place of birth ...Chicago.Ill.
4. Date of birth ..Aug.22,1907............   Age last birthday.29.
5. Description of applicant:
   Weight.145.......Height.5'6".....Color hair Red.........Color eyes..Grey.
6. Citizenship..American.......................Race....White........
   If alien, what country?.....................................   (White) (Negro)
7. If alien, and only declaration of intention to become a citizen of the United States has been filed, state the following:
   (a) Serial number of declaration..................Date of filing...........
   (b) State, city and court in which filed...

8. Have you previously applied for any class of pilot's license? No
   If so, list the following information:
   (a) Class of license...
   (b) Were you approved or disapproved?..........
   (c) Date examined...
   (d) Place of examination...
   NOTE.—If examined more than once, answer for last examination only.
9. Do you now hold a pilot's license or a student pilot's permit issued by the Department of Commerce Yes
   If so, state class and numberStudents..pilot.permit...
10. If application is for a limited commercial pilot's license, name:
    (a) Airport or field from which you will operate as base ..Belevedere..Airport.
    (b) Address of base ..West..Palm..Beach..Florida..................
11. Date of last physical examination ..Sept.21,1936.
12. Education, including air courses:Private Tutor, Grade School,Chicago Conservatory of Music(Graduate)Albany Law School(Graduate) One year P.G.Columbia University. 3 month course harmony and Orchestration,Eastman School Music, Rochester New York.

Application must be sworn to before a notary public, accompanied by two identical photographs, 1½ x 1½ inches in size, showing head and shoulders only, and submitted to the nearest Department of Commerce inspector.
Unless all questions are answered, it will be necessary to return the application.
STUDENT PILOT APPLICATIONS may be secured from an authorized Department of Commerce medical examiner at the time of accomplishing the physical examination.

(OVER)

11—9784

Application for Pilot's License

(2) 160

13. Experience as pilot, that is, as the sole operator of the controls and in command of aircraft in flight.

 (a) Name flying fields where you received instructions and their locations....Belevedere..Airport
  West..Palm..Beach..Florida..

 (b) Name instructors and give dates..W.R.Lemon..Sept...1934..to..Sept...1936.

 (c) Solo hours in last 60 days 38!15". Solo hours in last year 51!25" Total solo hours 51!25"
 (d) Name fields where you have operated; give dates and names of employers..................

 (e) Are you applying as a graduate of an Approved School? No.
  Name of Approved School...
  Course from which graduated (Tran., LC., Pri., Solo)...................
  Is certificate of graduation attached?.................................
  Total dual hours..................... Total solo hours................
 (f) Name types flown and hours in each..... Bird 0-2 – 30 hrs.   Fairchild – 1 hr.
  Taylor Cub – 2.0 hrs.
  Am. Eagle – 15 min.

14. Experience and training on aircraft engines, giving types with which familiar and length of experience on each
 KinnerK-5 Wright J-5 Continental A40-3
 Kinner Two years. Assisting with overhaul and general
 Wright J-5 1 month maintainance.
 Cont. 2 months.

15. Experience as to airplane structure and rigging, giving types with which familiar and length of experience
 on each. Bird American Eagle Challenger
 Taylor Cub
  assisting with overhauling and general maintainance.

16. Have you read the Air Commerce Regulations? Yes.

17. AFFIDAVIT:
  State _Florida_ ⎫
  County _Palm_ ⎬ ss.
       ⎭

I hereby swear that the statements contained in this application are true.

Dated this ___22 nd___ day of _September_, 1936

      Dowely W. Brink.
        (Signature)

Subscribed and sworn to before me this __22 rd__ day of _September_, 1936

     Lenora M. O'Connell
        Notary Public.

My commission expires _June 13_, 1938

DIRECTIONS

 1. Application for only one class of license may be made on this form.
 2. The physical examination must be taken before an authorized medical examiner of the Department of Commerce. In case applicant is a regular or reserve pilot of the Army, Navy or Marine Corps, he may instead submit a copy of an Army or Navy physical examination for flying, if such examination has been made within the last six (6) months. Certificate of the result of such examination will not be accepted.
 3. The applicant must furnish a licensed aircraft for the tests involved.

U. S. GOVERNMENT PRINTING OFFICE 1931   11—9724

Application for Pilot's License (pg.2)

49

Brink, while leaving, once again, the identity of the father of her alleged four sons unexplained and "private."

At this point, after four or five years of on again-off again motivation, I caution readers against a sense that at any point in my pursuit of Dot's story, this has been an easy climb. Over many years there have been frequent, often lengthy periods of lassitude, disappointment and enervation when missing elements of her life story seemed unreachable, inexplicable, even probably unknowable. Dot's true parentage, details of her birth, her education, and the mystery of her alleged sons were major missing links which I was unable to verify with my best efforts. I might have given up then, but again, seemingly out of the blue, another instance of unanticipated details and sources appeared, and their astounding materialization served to reinvigorate the climb. Fortune smiled on me in the form of an unexpected connection.

CHAPTER **8**

REVELATION—
Now who was she?

THUS CAME A second, electrifying "eureka" moment, courtesy of the great-granddaughter of Dorothy's adoptive parents, the Martins.

In early 2012, six years into my Dot Lemon quest, I received an unexpected phone call from the above mentioned great-granddaughter, who told me she had seen a blurb in the EEA Vintage Airplane magazine of November 2011 soliciting information on my behalf about Dot Lemon. She identified herself as a member of the Martin family, saying she knew that Dot Lemon was her grandfather's adopted sister.

As a result of the EEA Vintage Airplane magazine's blurb about Dot Lemon, this Martin family member had been motivated to peruse some material in an old desk inherited from her own grandmother. She kindly told me she would be going through the material, and promised to send anything that looked to be related. I gave her my email address and said how much I appreciated her phone call, not really believing there would be much of interest forthcoming.

Yet, on April 5, 2012, I received an email from this lovely lady which said, "I had to scan this as two documents since it is more

Milwaukee County Court.

In the Matter of the Adoption of

Rachel Reque

by Albert A. Martin

and Clara Martin _____, his wife.

Upon reading and filing the petition of Albert A. Martin

and Clara Martin _____, his wife, from which it appears that the said

Rachel Reque

is a child of Josephine Reque _____ and

_____, his wife

_____; that said Rachel Reque _____ is an infant

under the age of fourteen years, and was born on the 22nd day of August

A. D. 1906.; _____

That said Albert A. Martin and Clara Martin

are desirous to adopt said infant as their child; and said Hon. Neele B. Neelen having

been duly appointed special representative

_____ the _____ of said child, having

given his consent in writing to such adoption, and this Court being satisfied of the identity

and relations of the persons, and that said petitioners are of sufficient ability to bring up, and furnish

suitable nurture and education for said child, having reference to the degree and condition of its par-

ents, and that it is proper that such adoption shall take effect;

52

𝔍𝔱 𝔦𝔰 𝔒𝔯𝔡𝔢𝔯𝔢𝔡, That from and after the date hereof, said Rachel Reque

shall be deemed to all legal intents and purposes the child of the petitioners Albert A.

Martin and Clara Martin his wife.

and that the name of said child be changed to Dorothy Martin

according to the prayer of said petition.

Dated this 8th day of October 1907

In Duplicate.

By the Court,

John C Karel

County Judge.

Dot Lemon (Martin) Adoption Document

than letter size." I could not believe what I was seeing; the hair rose on the back of my neck. The scanned image was a copy of the original Dot Lemon adoption document,[26] dated the 8th day of October 1907, issued by the Milwaukee County Court. What a gift, one I had never, ever contemplated receiving. Adoption documents are notoriously difficult, and often even impossible to uncover. Now, unforeseen distant horizons regarding my project became reachable. A whole new chapter in the life of Dot Lemon, totally unimagined, remained to be discovered.

The adoption document that the Martin family member had attached in the email contained new information. According to this adoption document, a girl, Rachael Reque, is listed as the child of Josephine Reque. "This child was born on the 22nd day of August AD 1906 and then adopted by Albert A. Martin and his wife Clara Martin." A fit! So began another cycle in my pursuit of Dot Lemon's life odyssey.

To open this new path of inquiry, I began with the Norwegian American Genealogical Center and Naeseth Library, located in Madison, Wisconsin. The library confirmed the Reque family origins in the Voss area of Norway, and established that Josephine Reque and her brother John left that part of Norway from Bergen in 1904. Throughout her life, Dot claimed Danish, but never Norwegian heritage! Nowhere in my research had I previously found any reference by Dot to Norway or a Norwegian mother. While this piece of the puzzle seemed to fit, I had to wonder why things with Dot never matched up exactly. Still, I was highly motivated to continue the research.

Further digging showed that in May of 1904 the passenger ship "AURANIA" out of Liverpool, England arrived in New York. On board were Gurine Josephine Reque from the Voss area of Norway, along with her brother John J. Reque (also spelled Rekve). They were listed on the ship's manifest as "servants," showing an uncle, Sjur J. Reque, living in Chicago, Illinois. One Sievert (Sjur) Reque is listed in the 1910 Chicago City Directory at 1907 N. 40th Ave.

Subsequently, members of the Reque line, both in the United States and Norway, generously assisted me with both their time and invaluable knowledge of the Reque family history and origins. Most curiously, and only incidentally, Dorothy's WWI pilot/flight instructor, Major Merrill K. Riddick, was identified by my Reque family interlocutors as distantly related to the Reque family line, which includes Dorothy's birth mother Josephine. Was this another coincidence in the arc of Dorothy's life belief in astrology?

The name Rekve is probably derived from two words in Norwegian: the first one means tearing (apart) and the second refers to some pasture or cultivated land. The name Reqve was used to describe the area where the river—when flooded—tore apart good land. Emigrants from this area in Norway were known as the "Vossings." Thus it may be that Josephine and her brother, the Rekve "Vossings", were predestined to depart from their native land, "torn apart" from their home as it were. Dot would likely have claimed this was due to their astrological signs and data!

It seems probable that Uncle Sjur, already an established businessman in Chicago, had offered to help his niece and nephew in the adventure of emigrating to the new world, and assist them in getting settled and finding employment. While it is not known with certainty where Josephine obtained employment, her self-described status as a "servant" points to the likelihood that she would have obtained employment by one of Chicago's wealthy elite families.

According to popular folklore from this era, many young female émigrés to the United States either arrived pregnant, with or without husbands, or became pregnant shortly after arriving to a new, unfamiliar place far from their previous homes and family. This may well have been the situation of the recently arrived Josephine Reque, Dorothy's birth mother.

Harking back to Dorothy's adoptive father the Rev. Albert Alvin Martin, and the discovery of the foundling twins, Dorothy and her deceased brother, where in 1904 the Rev. Martin was a Special Agent at the Children's Home Society in Milwaukee, Wisconsin. The work of the Society was to place dependent children in approved private family homes. As noted previously, according to written records of Rev. Martin's descendants, "my grandfather worked for an orphanage in Milwaukee, WI. While there they adopted a baby girl, found with a twin brother left in a clothes basket on the steps of the orphanage." The baby boy, named Randolph, died on December 15, 1906.

The Illinois Home and Aid Society

The Illinois Society was originally founded in 1883 to aid orphaned and abandoned children, and it sought to place these children in private family homes rather than institutions. With expansion, the name was changed to the National Children's Home Society and in 1897, it became finally the Illinois Children's Home and Aid Society. Among the names in a listing of Board of Directors about 1907 (Dorothy's adoption year), is that of Mrs. John Borden (Ellen Waller Borden), a member of the socially prominent and wealthy Borden family, residents of the so called "Chicago Gold Coast." Active in many charity and fundraising efforts, she was Chairman of the Case Committee of the Illinois Children's Home and Aid Society. Mrs. Ellen Borden lived at 1020 Lake Shore Drive. This is the address listed in Dorothy's birth certificate, even while it showed her parents as the mysterious Whitneys.

While any connection between the Illinois Children's Home and Aid Society and the Children's Home Society in Milwaukee is never explicitly mentioned, both were active in their respective neighboring states during the 1907 time frame, and a significant percentage of both their émigré immigrant populations came from Northern Europe and Scandinavia.. Their stated purposes were to aid orphaned and abandoned children. Thus, I could see an ostensible connection between these two adoption Societies, where Dot listed the Borden address of Lake Shore Drive, the home of Mrs. Borden, Chair of the Illinois Society, as her Whitney family residence, and then Milwaukee, home of the Martins, he Special Agent in the neighbouring Milwaukee Society, as her childhood residence. But what of the Whitneys? In other documentations, the same Lake Shore Drive address was given as the Whitney address.

It should be noted that Dorothy and her twin brother were not then true "foundlings," in that their birth mother Josephine Reque was known, or became known at the time of Dorothy's adoption. This has led me to believe the discovery on the "steps" of the orphanage, and subsequent adoption, were probably arranged by unidentified, but interested third parties. Could this mean that the abandonment which led to the adoption of Dorothy had been carefully orchestrated? At this juncture, I perceived a thread tying the Whitney and Borden family names to the Chicago Lake Shore Drive address, possibly revealing who might have been the unidentified but interested parties involved in what appears to have been an arranged adoption.

CHAPTER 9

Dorothy's Natural Mother and Childhood, Revisited

JOSEPHINE REQUE, DOT'S birth mother according to the adoption papers, appears in the 1910 US Census married to a Mr. John G. Dellinger and residing in Dane, Wisconsin. Josephine's whereabouts between 1904, date of her arrival to the US, and 1910 are not known. Reviewing the documents once more, I still felt most sure that indeed her Uncle Sjur had helped her find employment in Chicago as a servant in the home of a wealthy family, a situation quite common with newly arrived young women emigres to the US in this era.

Throughout her life, Dot named the "Whitneys" as her birth parents. Referring back to Dot's 1936 and 1942 declarations regarding her "Whitney" parentage, it is useful to note again that their 1000/1020 Lake Shore Drive address on Chicago's Gold Coast is the same address as that of Mrs. John Alden Borden (Ellen Waller Borden), executive of the Illinois Children's Home and Aid Society. However, although the Whitneys were another prominent family in Chicago during those years, there is no record of a Whitney family living at this particular address, nor indeed of an Albert Arlington Whitney married to a Dorothy Catherine Hubbell. Dot had claimed her Whitney parents residence (Lake Shore Dr. in Chicago), actually that of the Borden family. This is where her birth mother (Josephine Reque) may have worked as a servant of the Borden family, active supporters of the Illinois Children's Home and Aid Society as well as the Bush Temple of Music in Chicago, the latter being where Dorothy claimed to have studied. The pieces of the puzzle were all more and more of one piece, too coordinated to be merely coincidental.

The Borden Family and Bush Temple of Music

According to Dot's Gale Research biography, probably filled in by Dot herself, she claimed to have studied for years at the Bush Conservatory of Music in Chicago, Illinois. Her curriculum included academics and music tutors.

Located on the corners of Clark Street and Chicago Avenue, the Bush Temple, the building where the Conservatory was located, was constructed in 1901. The building is still there today. This was the only conservatory in Chicago offering residential facilities for women and men students, beginning in the early 1920s. In addition to the music curriculum, the school also offered courses in languages, dancing, dramatic arts, expression, and stagecraft. Dorothy claimed to have studied there for five years, prior to having departed for New York State with her adopted family, the Martins. The 1920 census shows the Martin family still in Nebraska, but Dorothy may have been away at school in Chicago, at the Bush Conservatory between 1920 and 1926, as she claimed. Bush Conservatory records for this period are not complete, and Dorothy's actual attendance has not been documented. However, her Martin family sisters said that when living in New York State with the family, Dorothy "could dance and play the piano well." Julie Rive-King, famed Chicago pianist, who studied under Franz Liszt, began teaching in Chicago early in the twentieth century. For many years she was on the faculty of the Bush Conservatory, and while unsubstantiated, may well have contributed to Dot's alleged concert piano abilities. Further lending credibility to her oft-noted musical talents, in a September 1936 application Dot claimed a three-month course in harmony and orchestration at the Eastman School of Music, Rochester New York, where Dorothy appears to have been from about 1926-30. The jacket of Dot's book "One-One" carries laudatory remarks by famed composer Vittorio Giannini, Julliard School of Music, another example of Dot's well-known or famous contacts, and further evidence of her musical appreciation.

The Bush Conservatory's sponsors were an interesting cast of characters. The patrons included the rich residents of Lake Shore Drive, counting among them the aforementioned Mrs. John Borden, first wife of John Borden, owner of the 1020 Lake Shore Drive residence, later claimed by Dorothy as her Whitney birth parents' residence.

It should be noted that the Martin family was not wealthy, and was not living in the Chicago area during the period (1921-1925) when Dorothy said she had been at the Bush Conservatory. If she did indeed study there as she claimed, she almost surely received financial support from other than her adopted family, the Martins. It appears to be more than coincidental that she often listed her alleged parents' (the Whitneys) address in Chicago as 1020 Lake Shore Drive, the address of Mrs. John Alden Borden, as described above. Dot's oft-cited reference to the Chicago Lake Shore address ties her notionally to the Whitney and Borden families. It thus seems that either family might have been a financial contributor to Dorothy, further leading to speculation as to why: was there possibly a birth connection?

Dorothy never publicly identified her birth father as a member of the wealthy and prominent Whitney family, although the Whitney name appears on her birth certificate, and passport application signed by her. While she acknowledged the fact that she was the adopted daughter of Pastor and Mrs. Albert Martin, she often hinted that her biological father was a wealthy and prominent man from Chicago. She also included the surname "Requa (Reque)" as one of her claimed Whitney mother's maiden names, indicating she probably knew the identity of her actual birth mother, Josephine Reque, from Norway. Her response in those days to any further inquiries on the matter was that her past was "private." Yet one more of her lifelong enigmas!

A newspaper search, however, turned up the following story. This material is quoted from the 1 August 1943 Miami Daily News- Record, Miami, Oklahoma interview of Dot by Kathleen Koepnick.[27]

"Mrs. Lemon was Dot Whitney. As a charming member of that circle her career was pre-ordained. Finishing school, a debutante's year, then the 'right' places at the 'right' seasons. Since her movements and her associates would be within the circumference of New York's 100 a brilliant social marriage would come, followed by a society existence among the smart set of the East's gold coast.

From the moment Dot focused on an airplane all that was passed over. In no time at all she was swapping her presentation at the Court of St. James for a chance to help around the airdromes at New York fields. Sheer necessity might have cut short her career, for, in the manner of the day, her family disinherited her. An uncle whose pioneering had been thwarted into a brilliant legal career was her only rooter. He listened to her dreams without scathing comments upon her 'itinerant aviator friends."

While there is scant evidence of Dorothy's self-claimed Whitney family parentage, she used the Whitney name on numerous official documents. Her use of the Lake Shore Drive address in Chicago would seem to link her more closely to the Borden family than to any Whitney family connection, although as two wealthy and prominent families, the Bordens and Whitneys most likely crossed paths both socially and in other

Miami Daily New Rocord, August 1943

enterprises. Moreover, there is no apparent reason for Dorothy to have picked the Whitney name for her parentage other than that it may have been partially true.

There was an A.A. Whitney, in fact. The 1880 United States Census shows an Albert A.A. Whitney, age six months, living with the family of Alonzo Whitney, in Coulterville, Randolph, Illinois. This Whitney[28] would have been about twenty-six in 1906, the year of Dorothy's (Rachael Reque) birth. Perhaps he grew up to be the young father of Dorothy, and then later a successful member of society who may have been identified implicitly, but not legally as her birth father. Dot's introduction of her alleged Whitney parentage first occurred in her 1936 application for Social Security. The first explicit hint of wealthy parentage occurs in the Kenneth Stratton "sketch" of Dot's introduction to flying, (reviewed in Chapter 2) written years later (circa 1940), in which Stratton says: "Dot gave up wealth and social position to embark upon a career." The above Miami Daily News- Record article by Kathleen Koepnick was written in 1943.

What might have prompted Dot to introduce Whitney parentage in 1936, and to reinforce the story in both the 1940 Stratton article and the 1943 Koepnick interview, remains subject to various imaginable explanations, all of which led me to continued possibilities of intrigue and conjecture. Dot's claimed four sons, if they existed, would have been born prior to 1936, when Dot first claimed Whitney parentage for herself. Did Dot know or suspect her Whitney parentage early on, but only when four children appeared with a need for a respectable background, to perhaps include some financial support for the boys, did she decide to reveal her claimed Whitney parentage? Well, we know the name of Dot's birth mother, according to adoption papers but, alas, her birth father's name remains the subject of broad speculation.

1880 United States Federal Census

Name:	Alonzo Whitney
Age:	42
Birth Date:	Abt 1838
Birthplace:	New York
Home in 1880:	Coulterville, Randolph, Illinois, USA
Dwelling Number:	229
Race:	White
Gender:	Male
Relation to Head of House:	Self
Marital Status:	Married
Spouse's Name:	Margret J. Whitney
Father's Birthplace:	New York
Mother's Birthplace:	New York
Occupation:	Farmer

Household Members:	Name	Age
	Albert A. A. Whitney	6/12
	Alonzo Whitney	42
	Margret J. Whitney	40
	Armenia M. Whitney	15
	William G. Whitney	13
	John C. Whitney	9

Source Citation: Year: *1880*; Census Place: *Coulterville, Randolph, Illinois*; Roll: *244*; Family History Film: *1254244*; Page: *598C*; Enumeration District: *106*

1880 U.S. Census, Albert A.A. Whitney

CHAPTER 10

Belvedere Field and World War II

DOT LEMON WAS fully embarked on her career as a pilot by 1936. In that same year, Lemon had leased Belvedere Field, Florida, with Dorothy C. Brink listed as Treasurer/Instructor and Leon P. Brink listed as Pilot/Instructor. Following her documented marriage to William Richmond 'Doc' or 'Prof' Lemon on 4 April 1937, Dorothy decided to become known as simply "Dot" Lemon. She and her husband were the proprietors of the W. R. Lemon Inc. Flying Service at Belvedere Field, later to become incorporated into the West Palm Beach International Airport complex, along with the nearby Morrison Field.

Dorothy Martin, Leon Brink, and Lemon, now together at Belvedere Field in Florida, had been previous associates at Hayes Field in Cicero, New York where Dorothy (Martin) had become sales manager of the American Eagle aircraft agency in 1929/30.

According to her Contemporary Authors biography, during her time in Florida (1932? – 1941), Dot was very active in teaching people to fly, developing flight patterns for visual airport approaches, and teaching over the radio (Station WJNO "Skyways and Byways" West Palm Beach), through which she taught over 300 students a course in meteorology, each one passing a government exam with an average of 75 percent or higher. The same biography said, "It is a matter of Government Record that she never had a student fail either a flight test or written examination."

Among her many other activities, Dot laid claim to having been the first person to intentionally fly into the eye of a hurricane for weather information, off the coast of Florida in a Stinson Reliant airplane, in 1932. The fact of and possible date for this event have not been verified. However, there were Florida hurricanes in 1932, '36 and '37 that she could have flown, and it is known that Dick Lemon had a Stinson aircraft in his use at the Belvedere airport in 1936. To attempt this would not have been out of character for Dot, who also claimed that she had charted the path of a 1937 hurricane from Turk's Island to Canada, timing the center of disturbance. She said her figures were within four minutes of disturbance arrival; her barometric pressure forecasts were within .00003 limits; and her calculations of wind velocities and gust velocities were exact. This young woman of many talents, seemingly destined to join New York's social elite, had indeed "succumbed" to aviation.

As to the training that helped her become an accomplished pilot and navigator, Dot mentioned in the same ContemporaryAuthors biography that she received her celestial navigator's degree in 1929 from the Weems Co., located in Annapolis, Maryland.

Taken from Wikipedia:

Celestial navigation, also known as astronavigation, is the ancient and modern practice of position fixing that enables a navigator to transition through a space without having to rely on estimated calculations, or dead reckoning, to know their position.

INSTRUMENT FLYER TO VISIT—Dot Lemon, blind-flying expert, will visit San Antonio Feb. 8-9 as a guest of Texas 99's. She will be an honor guest at the women's aviation convention at the Gunter Hotel.

Instrument Flying Favored
By Well-Known Woman Pilot

Aerobatics and racing rate far below the technicalities of instrument flying in the opinion of Dot Lemon, Oklahoma City pilot who will attend the women's aviation convention here Feb. 8-9.

In 20 years in the aviation business, Mrs. Lemon has flown everything from rickety "Jennies" to huge DC-3 transports. Putting the newer ships through their paces on instruments has interested her most.

Her work in blind flying and meteorology have been recognized internationally by aviation writers, who declare her name has become a "legend of precision flying" among instrument pilots.

An instrument expert herself, she has taught her specialty to more than 800 students.

At the women's aviation meet, to be held at the Gunter Hotel, will be more than 200 women pilots from throughout the Southwest. The meeting was called by Texas members of the 99's, international women's flying club.

Gasoline Retail
Price Up 1 Cent

The retail price of gasoline was raised one cent by most San

"EARLY BIRDS"
APPLY FOR 1947
VEHICLE PLATES

San Antonio Express 1947 News Article

And from the Nautical Almanac:

"...the science of navigating by the celestial bodies (stars, Sun, planets and Moon)."

She also claimed to have taken courses in meteorology and navigation at Syracuse University from May to September 1929. Despite a lack of confirmation regarding these studies, much is written in acknowledgement of her professional stature. Among these articles,[29] one in particular from the San Antonio Express dated 2 February 1947, described Dot as "having been recognized internationally as a legend of precision flying among instrument pilots, and a leading navigation expert of that era." When combined with her future presidency of the Institution of Navigation in 1961, these are matters of public record strongly attesting to her celebrated navigation skills.

Leon P Brink, Revisited

While in association with Dot and her husband at Belvedere Field in Florida, and previously at Hayes Aviation in Cicero, New York, Leon P. Brink (whom Dot had claimed marriage to in 1927 and who may have been the father of her anonymous boys), had branched out into flying back and forth to the Bahamas. On one of these trips, in 1933 during Prohibition in the States, Brink earned brief notoriety for having survived fifty-two hours floating on an inner tube in the Gulf Stream. Brink's plane developed engine trouble thirty minutes after leaving West Palm Beach.[30] "I had a large automobile inner tube covered with canvas for a life preserver. As my plane settled on the water I inflated it fully and took a small hand pump with me to keep it well filled. After spending two days and two nights [in the water], getting hungrier and thirstier, I saw the J.N. Pew tanker and she heard my calls for help." In 1935 both Leon Brink and Dot's legal husband, Dick Lemon, long associates,

FLIER'S LIFE IS SAVED BY TIRE

Aviator, Down at Sea, Keeps Alive For 52 Hours

PHILADELPHIA, Feb. 17—(UP) —A story of hunger, thirst and the menace of Gulf Stream sharks was related today by Leon Brink, 37, Miami, Fla., aviator, who clung to an inflated auto tire 52 hours after his plane was forced down off the Florida coast last Saturday.

Brink, who was picked up by the Sun Oil tanker, J. N. Pew, arrived in Marcus Hook carrying the tube and a small hand pump with which he had kept it afloat. "I was frightened at times when the sharks came too close," he admitted, "but they seemed to be more inquisitive than hungry."

Flying a two-seater biplane, Brink was bound from Miami to the Bahamas when motor trouble forced him down 30 miles off the Florida coast. The plane broke up in the heavy seas shortly after it struck the water. He was sighted Monday afternoon by Donald Arntz, second mate of the tanker. Captain John Pypeliuk, ordered a boat lowered and took the aviator aboard.

Theatres

AT THE STATE

Lili Damita, who plays the feminine lead opposite Warren Williams in the First National picture, "The Match King," which will be shown at the State theatre today was chosen as the one actress who could suitably interpret the role, after a careful weighing of the possibilities of all Hollywood's talent.

The selection of just the right ac-

Leon Brink Plane Crash

were involved in an illegal money order fraud. Lemon received a suspended sentence, while Brink was sentenced to twelve months in the county jail. His sentence was reduced because of his previous service in the Armed Forces in WWI. Daily News Standard, "Flier's Life Is Saved by Tire," Uniontown, PA, 17 February 1933.

Dot's World War II Service

By January of 1942 all private and non-military flying had been suspended within a radius of six miles around Morrison Field, which affected Belvedere Field where Dot and her husband based their flying operations. It is believed that Dick ("Doc") Lemon then became an advanced flight instructor for the USAAF within the Embry Riddle Flight School company, originally in Florida, then later in Texas in the mid-1940s. He and Dot were often separated for lengthy periods of time, each assigned to their own particular calls of duty. According to copies of personal letters[31] in my possession (provided by Martin family descendants), written in August 1942 by Dot to her older step-sister, Aura, Dot was at that time employed at the Harvey Young Airport in Tulsa, Oklahoma. She writes a letter to inform Aura that she is working for the Tulsa Aviation Service in charge of their Army Program (NFI-Not Further Identified). In this letter Dot says she has "been going to the school at Spartan learning to fly oceans blind by the Great Circle route," and is worried about being "called out" but hoping to stay longer as she "gets to see Prof. [her husband] once in a while." (He was at that time in Texas with Embry Riddle training new USAAF pilots.)

During WWII the Spartan School, referred to by Dot, operated three flight schools: one in Tulsa, one in Miami for British cadets, and one in Muskogee (Oklahoma) for Army Air Corps cadets. The one in Tulsa was split, with one-half for Army Air Corps cadets and one-half for civilian pilots. During WWII there were several female students in the civilian program, many of whom went on

to fly for the Women Air Force Service Pilots (WASP) or in the Civil Air Patrol (CAP). Spartan did provide "blind flying" training, and had since about 1930. Dot probably earned both her twin engine and blind flying certifications there in 1942. In an application to the Civil Aeronautics Authority[32] dated 1942 Dorothy stated she "had taken instrument instruction from Spartan School

48

UNITED STATES OF AMERICA
CIVIL AERONAUTICS AUTHORITY
WASHINGTON, D. C.

CERTIFICATE NO
35250

11·20·42

DISAPPROVED

INSPECTOR'S SIGNATURE

* Explain under REMARKS

**APPLICATION FOR AIRMAN (AIRLINE TRANSPORT PILOT)
CERTIFICATE OR INSTRUMENT RATING**

(Application must be printed or typed and submitted to an inspector of the Authority)

To the Civil Aeronautics Authority:

Application is made for **Instrument**
(Show airline transport pilot certificate or instrument rating)

1. Name **Dorothy** **Culver** **Lemon**
   (First name) (Middle name) (Last name)

2. Permanent mailing address **Harvey Young Airport** **Tulsa**
   (Street) (Post office)
   Oklahoma **Tulsa** **9-3632**
   (State) (County) (Telephone)

3. Principal business or occupation **Flying Instructor**
4. Place of birth **Chicago Ill**
5. Date of birth **August 22 1907** Age **35**
6. Description of applicant:
   Weight **133** Height **5'5½"** Color hair **Red** Color eyes **Gray** Sex **Female**
7. Nationality **United States** Race **White** Blue
   (Country)

8. If alien, and only declaration of intention to become a citizen of the United States has been filed, state the following:
   (a) State, city, and court in which filed
   (b) Date of filing (c) Serial number of declaration

9. Has any application submitted by you pursuant to the provisions of the Civil Air Regulations been denied within the past 2 years? **No** If so, state details, including:
   (a) Kind of application
   (b) Place and date of examination

10. Has any certificate or rating issued you pursuant to the provisions of the Civil Air Regulations been suspended or revoked within the past 2 years? **No** If so, state details

11. (a) Present pilot's certificate: Classification **Commercial** No. **35251**
    Ratings held **Instructor**
    (b) Radio license or permit held: No. **Rr-7-455** Class **Radio Telephone**
    Expiration date **Feb 8, 1945**

12. (a) Last physical examination **11-25-41** **Miami Fla** **Rufus J. Pearson**
    (Date) (Place) (Name of examiner)
    This examination was for **Commercial** pilot certificate
    (b) Have you any physical defects ordinarily disqualifying for the requested certificate or rating?
    None

13. Can you read, write, and understand the English language? **Yes**
    Academic education **Conservatory of Music. Law School.**

[OVER]

72

14. Do you speak English without such accent or impediment of speech as may interfere with two-wa radio conversation? **No**

15. Aeronautical education, including any special courses or knowledge that qualify you for this certif cate. Give dates and places **Have taken instrument instruction from Spart School Aeronautics- from July 1 to Nov 18 1942**

16. General aeronautical experience **Soloed May 1 1926 at Rochester N.Y. Have mad my living at flying since Nov. 1926**

17. Pilot time (in hours logged in accordance with the provisions of the Civil Air Regulations) :

	DAY	NIGHT	INSTRUMENT
Total	3845.00	200:00 - Total 4045:00	
Last 8 years	2445:05		
Last 60 days	174:10		23:20
Cross country	1800:00		

18. Instrument practice under simulated conditions (hours) : Hood **28:20** Link **15:00**

19. Record of instrument and radio navigation flight instruction received—

WHERE RECEIVED	INSTRUCTOR'S NAME	CLASS OF AIRCRAFT USED (2S, 3M, ETC.)	TYPE OF GROUND TRAINER USED
Spartan School	Manion Hodge	2S-145 Warner	Link

20. If engaged in commercial aviation, state name of employer, present position, and length of tim employed in such position **Harvey O. Young- Flight Instructor- 3 months**

21. Are you familiar with the current Civil Air Regulations applicable to the certificate applied for **Yes**

I CERTIFY that the above statements are true.

Date **11.28.42**

(Signature of applicant)

NOTE.—The applicant must furnish a certificated aircraft for the tests involved, with proper instruments and equip ment, and with dual controls installed.

REMARKS:

Civil Aeronautics Authority Application 1942

SEARCHING FOR DOT LEMON

From Webster's dictionary:

Noun: blind flying - using only instruments for flying an aircraft because you cannot see through clouds or mists etc.
...blind flying - using only instruments for flying an aircraft because you cannot see through clouds or mists etc.

She continues in her letter to step-sister Aura, "Maybe it won't happen but we are both resigned and prepared to not survive the war. The chances we have to take make it most improbable [that we should survive] but I guess we can't live forever. We've known love and fun, we've worked hard and tried to do our share, and it's no worse for us to die than thousands of others. So having it all settled in our minds we try not to think about it, but between you and me it's pretty hard sometimes." In another letter to "Aug" [sic] Dot says she has been drafted into the "Ferry Command" but had requested a deferment because she wanted to spend the winter close to "Prof."

"They say they are not drafting me as a woman but as a member of the Civil Air Patrol who has the qualifications they need. I have been on some pretty ticklish missions for the Civil Air Patrol ... which is after all a part of the Army Air Corp, but of course when they take you in they say 'Domestic Ferrying' but in three months' time you are sent 'where you can be of the most service' and me with my twin engine ratings and blind flying licenses means foreign duty."

Dot goes on in this letter to mention being "called to Canada for what reason I can't tell you," and that "he [husband Doc] gave me a thousand dollar Canadian Beaver coat for my birthday," saying "I want you to have everything you ever dreamed of because I don't think you'll be here long to enjoy it—or me either, so wear it good this winter Baby, there might not be another one." Dot comments, "Every time he comes back from one of those trips I cry with relief, and every time I come back it

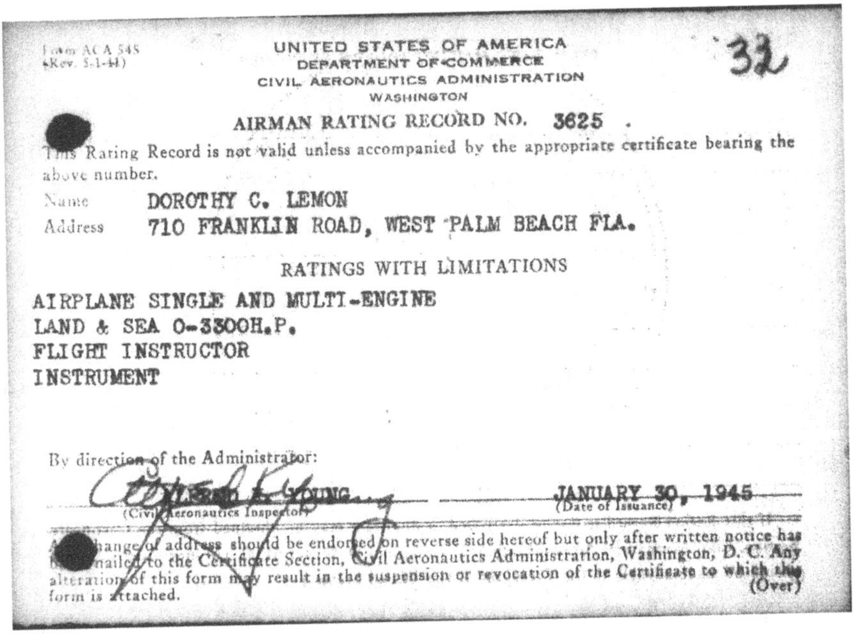

Form ACA 545
(Rev. 5-1-44)

UNITED STATES OF AMERICA
DEPARTMENT OF COMMERCE
CIVIL AERONAUTICS ADMINISTRATION
WASHINGTON

32

AIRMAN RATING RECORD NO. 3625 .

This Rating Record is not valid unless accompanied by the appropriate certificate bearing the above number.

Name DOROTHY C. LEMON
Address 710 FRANKLIN ROAD, WEST PALM BEACH FLA.

RATINGS WITH LIMITATIONS

AIRPLANE SINGLE AND MULTI-ENGINE
LAND & SEA 0-3300H.P.
FLIGHT INSTRUCTOR
INSTRUMENT

By direction of the Administrator:

(Civil Aeronautics Inspector) JANUARY 30, 1945 (Date of Issuance)

A change of address should be endorsed on reverse side hereof but only after written notice has been mailed to the Certificate Section, Civil Aeronautics Administration, Washington, D. C. Any alteration of this form may result in the suspension or revocation of the Certificate to which this form is attached. (Over)

Airman Rating Record

takes me a week to get the fear out of my stomach."

Dot's alleged WWII ferry activity and training is based on quite convincing anecdotal information from her personal letters, signed applications, newspaper articles, and family notes. There is a well-established WWII history of women pilots in the US serving as ferry pilots, pulling drones used for training gunnery practice, Civil Air Patrol, and more. Dot's multiple engine civil air ratings from the Department of Commerce[33] are a matter of record. In notes written by one of Dot's step-sisters, she says that during the war Dot flew back and forth to England. This latter statement seems improbable, as WWII women ferry pilots are not acknowledged as having flown the transatlantic routes, despite Dot's implication "of being sent where you can be of the most service."

In response to a query from her step-sister Aura as to whether Dot wouldn't like some "assurances of something beyond" if she didn't come back, Dot launches into a long written explanation of her life philosophy.

"Now the spirit? Well if anybody has ever amounted to anything at all or been kind or intelligent or useful and helped other people as they went along . . . well, their deeds and the things that they were just go on and on like echoes and ripples on water. They just live again in other people and they too can't be killed. No, I never read that anywhere or heard anybody else say it before I thought it out for myself. I figured it out years ago by myself. After I got it all straight in my mind I found out that many other people believed and had been taught almost the same thing in philosophy and science in universities. Of course they always teach the presence of a Supreme Being to which they worship conventionally in the chapel on Sundays. But to me the Supreme Being is the power to think. Intelligently. Also, the great motivating power of the universe is electricity. Not to push a button but the electrical impulses that radiate constantly all around us that are caused from friction of the billions of atoms and molecules that make up everything. It is what makes the radio waves. Maybe you get an idea what I mean if not here is a simpler explanation of what I think of a life beyond. Why should I have another life. If I don't do very well with this one what right have I to ask for another chance when I had all the chance in the world to make this one useful. Am I so selfish that I want to beg some Great Being to forgive my sins when it wouldn't help the ones I had sinned against, and if I knew I was committing the sins I should be punished by the laws of cause and result, and if I did not know I was committing them they were not sins? Why should I moon around about some future life of ease and perfect happiness that would be awaiting me when my heart stopped beating, when if I took the valuable time I wasted moaning and tried to make people happy around me, I should not only profit for myself but I should make my own happiness. I have always thought religion as we know it was such a selfish pursuit. It has always been, "Dear God gimme this and God if you will do this for ME I'll do this for you — Oh God please don't let anything happen to ME." If the human race would stop thinking about ME and think about the other fellow for a while the world wouldn't be in such a turmoil. But each and every race collectively and individually has always been taught to think about themselves. Of course I know that the law of self-preservation is the first law of life from a primitive stand-point but I thought that was what we were trying to get away from — a primitive standpoint."

Dot was thirty-five years old when she wrote this in 1942. Not exactly what one might expect from an illegitimate child of a Norwegian immigrant, baring her soul to a member of an unappreciative adopted family. I read this passage as an extraordinarily perceptive personal message written by Dot while she was likely under considerable mental war-related tension.

CHAPTER 11

Pylon Racing . . . Another Challenge

AFTER WWII, DOT Lemon was able to show off her notable talent as a pilot, and she was a welcome performer in exhibits of skill and speed. Dot became well known on the air racing circuit best represented by the National Air Races (NAR) held annually at Cleveland, Ohio. A February 1947 article in the San Antonio Express newspaper has Dot, described as an "Oklahoma blind-flying expert" and "top-ranking instrument pilot" attending a Texas Ninety-Nines convention of more than 100 Texan and Oklahoman women pilots.

The Ninety-Nines: International Organization of Women Pilots, was founded on November 2nd, 1929, at Curtiss Field, Valley Stream, New York, for the mutual support and advancement of women pilots. Another news article from August 27th, datelined Cleveland, says "Dot Lemon of Oklahoma City, red-haired and youthful looking mother of four sons in military service during the war, arrived in a slicked-up AT-6 Texan to fly in the Halle Trophy race for women....Miss Lemon finished fifth last year."

In another example of my researcher's occasional good fortune, a flying enthusiast sent me an actual photo of Dot's AT-6 with racing number 23. Dot appeared in multiple NAR races and events in Cleveland, most notably in 1946 and 1948.

The 2011-2012 exhibit "Dot Lemon...Curse of an Aviatrix" at the International Women's AIR & SPACE Museum (IWASM) noted:

"In 1948 she then took part in the Kendall Trophy Race, a 75 mile closed-course race with 15 mile laps." San Antonio Express, "Instrument Flying Favored by Well-Known Woman Pilot," San Antonio, TX, 2 February 1947.

"Lemon finished with an excellent time that was good enough to win equivalent races in years prior; however, 1st place was taken by Grace Harris in a record breaking performance at 235 mph. Not only did first place elude Dot, but 2nd place as well. She lost in an epic battle for 2nd to Katherine 'Kaddy' Landry by an average of .08 miles per hour. Kaddy was an acrobatic performer, and maneuvered into a dive at the last moment to pick up speed and edge out Dot." Dot did place third at 219 mph and won $750.

A press account dated April 3rd, 1949 in Houston, Texas announced: "on July 3-4, Dot Lemon will attempt to capture for America the world's three kilometer air speed record. Mrs. Lemon, who moved here recently from New York City, said the National Aeronautics Association has approved the dates. She plans to use the modified P-51 'Beguine' in making the record breaking attempt." The 'Beguine' was re-designed by its owner, J.D. Reed, Houston Beechcraft dealer, and North American Aviation, to exceed any speed yet reached by a propeller-driven craft.

"Exact time of the speed try will be determined by weather conditions. The three-kilometer record of 469 miles per hour currently is held by a German, Fritz Wendel, and has been foreign-held more than 25 years."

CHARLES TUPPER ASSOCIATES

News Release

FOR PUBLICATION OR RADIO USE SUNDAY APRIL 3, 1949

Houston, Texas -o- The country's top-ranking woman pilot, Dot Lemon of Houston, Texas, will attempt to capture for America the three-kilometer world speed record, the most important now held by a foreign flier.

The present record of 469 miles per hour was set ten years ago by Fritz Wendel, a German, flying a Messerschmidt 109. His mark has not been touched since. In a try at the course a year and a half ago, Jacqueline Cochran established a women's record of 413 m.p.h.

Mrs. Lemon is confident that the "Beguine" a modified P-51 in which she will make the speedrun, can top the all-time German speed by a good margin.

The "Beguine" was re-designed by its owner, J. D. Reed, Houston Beechcraft dealer, and North American Aviation, to exceed any speed yet reached by a propeller-driven craft. Its potential is unknown, since no pilot has yet let it out to the limit, but aviation experts here who have observed its performance believe it to be the fastest known.

Under the name "Houston International Air Speedrun", the flight will be made over a precision-timed course now being prepared here by direction of the National Aeronautics Association, which has authorized Class A rating.

P.O. BOX 2242   **HOUSTON 1, TEXAS**   C-0665

Air Speed Record Article

80

However, Dot never validated the event with the proposed venue, and other obstacles arose to prevent her from ever actually flying for the record.

Charles Tupper Associates,[34] Press Release C-0665, Houston, TX, 3 April 1949.
Prior to moving to Houston in 1949, Dot held an executive aviation position with the Petroleum Industries Company with offices in New York and Houston. A personal correspondence note dated 3 June 1948 shows her New York address as 70 Park Avenue, New York City.

Aviation Recognition

The IWASM in Cleveland, Ohio presented "Dot Lemon, Curse of an Aviatrix," an exhibit which ran from October 2011 through January 2012 in Cleveland, Ohio. As part of the IWASM exhibit for the 2014 Cleveland Air Show, IWASM[35] featured a short color film of Nancy Corrigan at the 1948 Women's Pylon Race, starring none other than Dot Lemon herself! As an aside, it must be said that Dot detested the term "aviatrix," something she did mention in several interviews. For her there was no gender distinction between pilots. Either you were, or were not, a genuine, well-qualified pilot.

The following is an excerpt written by Matt Sisson, from the IWASM monograph which accompanied the exhibit.

"Dot Lemon was a very accomplished pilot, and a pioneer for women in a field dominated by men. From allegedly being the first person to deliberately fly into the eye of a hurricane to obtain weather information, to becoming the president and founder of the 1st Chapter of Florida 99's in 1940. Dot Lemon was, at one point in time, regarded as the best instrument pilot in America."

"What remains to be said is that Dot Lemon seemed to live in a shroud of bad luck throughout her life. This, combined with a relative lack of indisputable evidence to document her life, portrays a story of mystery and intrigue. Her book "One-One" is a fictional allegorical tale about an airplane from the perspective of the plane itself. Dot describes it as 'a fantasy ... a composite of all the airplanes that have ever flown and all the airplanes which will ever fly.' Although Dot Lemon clearly stated that her book was a complete work of fiction, pieces of the story allude to her complicated life as a female and as an aviator."

CHAPTER **12**

Illness, Music, and Literary Parable

FROM ROUGHLY 1953-1963 Dot was seriously ill, suffering from complications associated with peritonitis from a ruptured appendix, leaving her legally blind and often bed-ridden. This followed almost immediately completion of her book entitled "One-One", variously described on her book's jacket cover as "a profound work, disguised as a simple little tale . . . a great story of life, death and resurrection, beautifully and poetically told." Famed composer Vittorio Giannini of the Juliard School of Music had the following to say about this book on the book's jacket cover:

> "Dot Lemon's book at first reading is a delightful story full of fantasy and allegory, yet it has a strange fascination that invites re-readings. On doing so one begins to understand the rocklike faith, the warm and generous love of humanity, the strength, the compassion and tenderness that lie in the deep meaning of this book."

"One-One" was written in 1953, but only published ten years later, in 1963, as a result of her illness and blindness.

Dot claimed that the complications were the result of an over-dose of sulfa drugs. Her eyesight was partially restored some seven years later in what was described as a near miraculous operation. This feat was performed in California by Dr. Robert Ware, allegedly the youngest man to have headed the Ophthalmology Department at the Johns Hopkins medical center in Baltimore, MD.

The Foreword to Dot's book was written by Guy Murchie, author of "Music of the Spheres and Song of the Sky." Himself an accomplished navigator, Murchie says that the reader of 'One-One' "will find something of a biblical elementalness [sic] in this irrepressible tale which seems to be at once fairy story and saga, simultaneously naive and profound, in its strange, unconventional, ungrammatical, dreamy style that spells out a very genuine primitiveness."

As to the artwork on the jacket cover for "One-One," it was created and expressly painted for the book by Charles H. Hubbell, aviation's most famous artist. I have not been able to identify the tie between Dot and Hubbell, which nevertheless would seem to have represented more than a passing acquaintance. Dot also included the Hubbell name among her alleged Whitney mother's maiden names. Another example of Dot's long list of famous/infamous friends?

Music

Roger Dettmer was the acclaimed music, theater, and recordings critic of the Chicago American and Chicago Tribune for many years. In 2008 I met with Roger personally twice in Annapolis, Maryland following his retirement. Dot had been introduced to Roger in 1950 at the Cincinnati Symphony, which began a relationship of some seventeen years. Roger told me he was struck by her seeming clairvoyance, while he became an avid student and believer in astrology, introduced and taught to him by Dot. He said he was in awe of her, believing Dot

possessed extra-sensory perception (ESP), and described seeing birds landing on her shoulders on a balcony at the Beverly
Hills Hotel. She told him she was descended from the Queen
of Denmark, and that he, (Roger) had been her son in a previous life. In 1950 Dot would have been forty-three, Dettmer
twenty-three. This characterization of Dot by Roger Dettmer, a
real first-person source who knew her well, verifies her captivating personality, yet leaves unresolved some of the mystifying
details of her extraordinary life. For example, her claim to Royal
Danish ancestry seems to be an embellishment of her personal
history, given her almost certain knowledge of her birth mother's Norwegian origins.

Roger was instrumental in introducing Dot to several prominent individuals in the world of music at that time, one of
whom was Vittorio Giannini[36] of the Julliard School of Music
and world-famed composer of many works, including "The
Christus." Giannini authored a comment for the dust cover of
her book "One-One." Both Dettmer and Giannini were fellow
"Leos" along with Dot, (and myself).

Another introduction facilitated by Dettmer was to the long-
time (1947-58) Music Director of the Cincinnati Symphony
Orchestra, Thor Johnson. In April of 2015 I received an "out
of the blue" email from Mary Beth Brandt and her husband,
Meng-Kong Tham, a Malaysian musician who studied in the
United States under the sponsorship of Dr. Thor Johnson at
Northwestern University.

The following is an excerpt from Mrs. Brandt's email to me:

Dot Lemon was a friend of Dr. Johnson. In fact, Dr.
Johnson arranged for her to pick up my husband from
the airport in L.A., put him up for two nights and get him
to the train for his journey to Chicago. Johnson wrote a
letter of introduction to my husband in which he referred
to Dot Lemon as one of his 'dearest friends.' My husband

has vivid memories of this brief encounter because Mrs. Lemon was such a gracious hostess. He was a terrified 'fresh off the boater' college student, from modest means, in the USA for the first time. He spoke only halting textbook English. She warmly welcomed him, took him around the sights of L.A. and to his great delight, made sure to include the famous 'Hollywood Bowl,' an iconic site in the mind of this emerging musician. She also spoke to him about being a pilot. He still remembers her elegant home, and the plush carpeting in the bedroom. He was so grateful for the huge bowl of fresh fruit she left in the room which he entirely consumed, hungry after a long journey! He has never forgotten Mrs. Lemon's kindness.

This touching story reminded me of the warmth and compassionate Dot Lemon qualities of the 1970s dinners in our home in Venezuela.

Dettmer's relationship with Dot seems hard to define, although likely facilitated by Dot's musical training and noted accomplishments of piano and dancing. He, an already established music critic in his own right, seems to have been dominated by Dot's strong and magnetic personality. They were united by their mutual appreciation and love of music, as well as astrology. At one point in their friendship she persuaded Dettmer's father to invest $10,000 dollars in one of her ventures. However, the father later asked for and received his money back, stating he did not trust her. Referring to a trip that Roger and Dot took together to visit Chicago in 1967, Dettmer told me, "the city never seemed to be 'home' to her. There was no curiosity, no memories shared or evinced, no wish to see anything or anybody. Odd for one supposedly born there and a resident for many years."

Dettmer's conversations with me in Annapolis were based

on his belief in the accuracy of her birth certificate which he had seen, showing her birth in Chicago, assumedly born of Whitney parentage. His comments were thus valid based on what he believed to have been her life in Chicago as a Whitney. He never mentioned to me knowing anything about her adoption and birth circumstances. Then, sometime in 1967 Dot wrote Dettmer out of her life, for reasons Dettmer declined to discuss with me. He said Dot had told him that "if you ever tell anyone I am crazy, I will haunt you the rest of your life." I am pretty sure he believed her!

Dettmer's characterization of Dot Lemon as a clairvoyant and captivating personality stands in juxtaposition to her emerging prominence as an executive in the scientific world of the Institute of Navigation, a feature of her life that developed during the same time frame as did her relationship with Roger Dettmer. His knowledge of her as a friend was perhaps more similar to mine, when as her friend in later years, I had no idea of the many facets of her professional accomplishments as a pilot, author, entrepreneur and navigational expert.

CHAPTER 13

The Institute of Navigation (ION)

IN 2015 I received permission to access the Weems ION Collection at the Smithsonian National Air and Space Museum located at Dulles airport near Washington, DC. Among the many files I searched, there was ample material documenting Dot's varied and extensive roles in the ION, roles which culminated in her 1961 election to the ION Presidency.

In 1961 Dot Lemon[39] became the first female president of this very prestigious and scientific organization. How she came to be elected president of an organization whose membership at that time was composed of 99 percent male scientists of eminence with records of outstanding achievements in their respective fields, surely lends great credence to her ascribed brilliant mind and extraordinary accomplishments in the related fields of aviation and navigation.

The official stated purpose of the ION is as follows:

The Institute of Navigation, founded in 1945, is a non-profit professional society dedicated to the advancement of the art and science of navigation. It serves a diverse community including those interested in air, space, marine, land navigation and position determination.

INSTITUTE OF NAVIGATION

National Office

711 14th Street, N. W.

Washington 5, D. C.

1961 - 1962

PRESIDENT
MRS. DOT LEMON

EXECUTIVE SECRETARY
CAPT. I. E. RITTENBURG, C&GS (RET.)

CHAIRMAN OF THE EXECUTIVE COMMITTEE
CAPT. P. V. H. WEEMS, USN (RET.)

TREASURER
LT. COL. WILL O. BRIMBERRY, USAF

PAST PRESIDENTS
COLIN H. McINTOSH
GORDON A. ATWATER
REAR ADMIRAL GORDON McLINTOCK, USMS
DR. PAUL ROSENBERG
CAPTAIN P. V. H. WEEMS, USN (RET.)
DR. SAMUEL HERRICK
E. A. LINK
MAJOR GENERAL N. B. HARBOLD, USAF
REAR ADMIRAL R. W. KNOX, C&GS
GILES GREVILLE HEALEY
VERNON I. WEIHE
HENRY REMPT
CAPTAIN ALTON B MOODY, USNR
CAPTAIN I. E. RITTENBURG, C&GS (RET.)

VICE-PRESIDENTS
COMMANDER E. A. BEITO, USNR
SHERMAN MILLS FAIRCHILD
BRIG. GENERAL BERTRAM HARRISON, USAF
COLONEL EDWARD McKABA
BRIG. GENERAL P. C. SANDRETTO, USAFR
COMMISSIONER E. M. WEBSTER
CHARLES A. ZWENG

REGIONAL VICE-PRESIDENTS
G. D. DUNLAP (EASTERN)
DR. JOHN BELLAMY (WESTERN)

EDITOR OF NAVIGATION
JOHN DOHM

ADVERTISING MANAGER
G. D. DUNLAP

THURLOW AWARD COMMITTEE
PAUL SCHROCK, CHAIRMAN

BURKA AWARD COMMITTEE
JAMES L. DENNIS, CHAIRMAN

MEMBERSHIP
VERNON I. WEHIE

LATERAL COMMUNICATIONS
C. TOWNER FRENCH, CHAIRMAN

COUNCIL
DR. JOHN BELLAMY
WALLACE BRUDER
DR. JOSEPH CHAMBERLAIN
LT. COL. VICTOR C. CONWAY, USAF
DR. RAYNOR L. DUNCOMBE
W/CDR. KEITH GREENWAY, RCAF
HARRY B. HEISLER
REAR ADM. C. F. HORNE, USN (RET.)
MACLEAN KIRKWOOD
J. KESSING
JOHN LARSEN
JEROME LEDERER
DR. GENE R. MARNER
CAPTAIN T. C. MARTIN, USAF
FRANK E. McCLUNG
GUY MURCHIE
D. B. NICHINSON
COMMANDER LYLE C. READ, USN
CAPTAIN P. V. H. WEEMS, USN (RET.)
VERNON I. WEIHE
GRENVILLE D. ZERFASS

TECHNICAL COMMITTEE CHAIRMEN
AIR
CAPTAIN WILLIAM POLHEMUS

MARINE
REAR ADMIRAL CHARLES PIERCE, C&GS

SPACE
RAY W. HALLETT, JR.

The Institute of Navigation (ION)[38]

89

Although basically a national organization, its membership is worldwide, and it is affiliated with the International Association of Institutes of Navigation. The ION in the United States was founded at the University of California, Los Angeles, in 1945 by Capt. Philip Van Horn Weems (1899-1979) and Dr. Samuel Herrick, assistant professor of astronomy at UCLA. Capt. P.V.H. Weems, (USN ret) and his wife were founders of the Weems School of Navigation in 1927 after which he invented various navigation aids including the Mark II Plotter and the Second Setting Watch.

Dorothy, now Dot Lemon, claimed to have taken courses and studied meteorology, navigation and astronomy, as well as law, at several universities in the years between 1926 and 1930 or 1932. While these studies have not been documented, and her acquisition of expertise in these scientific fields continues to be one of her life's mysteries, it is a matter of public record that Dot became well-known and accepted as an expert in these same fields of knowledge, e.g., navigation, meteorology and astronomy. As a result of her ION membership, Dot became acquainted with and a life-long friend of the ION founder Capt. Weems and his wife Margaret. They exchanged personal letters for many years, in one of which Capt. Weems said he much anticipated dancing once again with Dot.

She began her affiliation with the ION in the late 1940s, and by 1952 she had been elected by the entire membership to the ION Council as a "Former Practicing Navigator." Dot, among the nearly all-male ION membership of distinguished scientists and technical experts, was elected ION Vice-President for the Western Region from 1955 to 1961. Another prominent ION member, Rear Admiral C.F. Horne, then President, General Dynamics, Electronics Division, became an associate and principal investor in a later Dot Lemon business venture.

In June 1960, as Western Region Vice President, Dot chaired the ION 16th Annual Meeting at the United States Air Force

Academy at Colorado Springs, Colorado. She received great acclaim for excellent leadership at this meeting, and for her overall exemplary organizational skills.

An article in the Pasadena, California Independent newspaper, dated 26 January 1961, reports a meeting of the Western Region ION in Pasadena to discuss "progress in scientific exploration from far below the earth's crust, and far on toward the most remote stars of the universe." The article says: "Mrs. Dot Lemon, Western Region Vice-President , will preside at the luncheon." The meeting was held at the California Institute of Technology (Caltech). It was during this period when Nobel Prize winning physicist, the late Dr. Robert A. Millikan of the California Institute of Technology, was often heard to remark that Mrs. Lemon possessed one of the finest and most remarkable intellects he had ever encountered.[37] Where did this intellect come from?

I was now acquainted with the apparent genius of Dot Lemon. As I thought back to our dinners in Venezuela, I wondered at the workings of her mind, the far-reaching vision of her grasp of the universe and her command of society and leadership.

CHAPTER 14

Venezuela and Gold Fever

YET ANOTHER GRAND enigma in Dot's remarkable life covers the period from about 1962 until 1986, when she died alone in poor health and destitute, in Caracas, Venezuela, buried in an anonymous gravesite. Extensive efforts by individuals, including this author and other employees in the State Department, have failed to locate or identify next of kin, other than descendants of her adoptive parents. The American Embassy in Caracas, Venezuela failed to recover her personal effects immediately following her death, which is a normal Consular function following the death of a US Citizen abroad. This is all the more regrettable as she was a "notable" person, whose personal papers and effects may well have shed light on the questions of her claimed sons, Venezuelan gold concessions and perhaps even her natural father. Dot remained in Venezuela throughout this period (1962-1986), until her death in 1986, in order to pursue her gold mining venture, with only occasional visits to the US.

The chapter of Dot's life involving the gold mines is a complicated story. In 1964, the Government of Venezuela under President Raul Leoni officially granted Dot Lemon twenty-five-year land concessions to gold mining properties in the Gran Sabana area of Venezuela. The properties, reputed to be among the potentially most valuable gold properties in the Western

Hemisphere, were named the "Cristinas." The official award of these mining concessions by the Venezuelan Government to Dot Lemon is recorded in the Official Gazette[40] (Gaceta Oficial) of the Republic of Venezuela dated 6 February and 27 August 1964.

Dot clearly had visions of great wealth resulting from her gold concessions. Mining publications in the mid-1990s estimated the potential wealth of those gold properties between 8 million and 20 million ounces of gold. At one point in her letters, Dot talked of buying race horses, a Caravel jet aircraft, and a vacation home on the Mediterranean where she would invite all her friends.

Dot wrote long letters from Venezuela detailing the difficulties attempting to develop her "Cristinas" gold concessions. In a letter dated 13 January 1962, apparently written to her mining company benefactors in the States, (never fully identified), she was particularly effusive in her praise for "Mr. McKenzie, my combination engineer, locator, geologist, guide and protector. He was from British Guiana, and when you walk in to the Ministry (Mines) here with him, all of the engineers and geologists make way with respect."

Dot went into considerable detail regarding her efforts to register her "Cristina" gold mining claims. In one passage she describes flying to a small town in the Venezuelan Grand Savannah named Guasipati, where they were to register claims. Her Mr. McKenzie spoke casually about the area's snakes, tigers, tarantulas, etc. Upon landing and a visit to the bathroom, she came to understand there was no running water in this small Indian town. An obliging local resident brought buckets of water for the plumbing fixtures. With the registration papers signed and filed in Guasipati for Cristinas One, Two, Three, and Four, Dot spoke of planning for a trip to the gold veins, some six hours by jeep into the mountains. "We have to cross the river on a barge of logs tied together, and after we get to the veins,

GACETA OFICIAL

DE LA REPUBLICA DE VENEZUELA

AÑO XCII — MES IV — Caracas: jueves 6 de febrero de 1964   Número 27.363

SUMARIO

Congreso Nacional

Convenio Postal Universal. — (Véase número 896 Extraordinario de la GACETA OFICIAL DE LA REPÚBLICA DE VENEZUELA, de esta misma fecha).

Ministerio de Relaciones Interiores

Resolución por la cual se confiere la Condecoración de la Orden Francisco de Miranda, en su Segunda Clase, al ciudadano Coronel Tomás Pérez Tenreiro, Agregado de las Fuerzas Armadas Nacionales a la Embajada de Venezuela en Roma.

Ministerio de Hacienda

Resolución por la cual se dispone tener en uso oficial la edición de setenta mil (70.000) juegos de formularios RC-1, cuyo precio por ejemplar se fija en cinco céntimos de bolívar (Bs. 0,05).

Ministerio de Fomento

Resoluciones relativas a registros de marcas de fábrica.

Ministerio del Trabajo

Resoluciones por las cuales se hacen dos nombramientos.
Resoluciones por las cuales se autoriza el funcionamiento de las Sociedades Cooperativas en ellas mencionadas.

Ministerio de Comunicaciones

Resolución por la cual se concede permiso para instalar y operar varias relaciones radioeléctricas.
Resoluciones por las cuales se concede renovación de permiso para continuar operando varias estaciones radioeléctricas.
Resolución por la cual se concede permiso a la empresa Línea Expresa Bolívar C. A., para explotar el servicio de expreso de pasajeros, de acuerdo a las condiciones en ella especificadas.

Ministerio de Justicia

Resolución por la cual se nombra Defensor Público Segundo de Presos de la Circunscripción Judicial del Estado Sucre, a la ciudadana Nelly Silva González de Angrisano y Suplentes a los ciudadanos Doctores Lourdes Josefina Blanco Villarroel y Angel Gostinett Marcano, Primero y Segundo, respectivamente.
Resolución por la cual se procede a aumentar a veinte mil bolívares la fianza, a razón que ha de otorgar al Registrador Subalterno del Distrito Perijá del Estado Zulia.
Resoluciones por las cuales se designan la Cárcel Nacional de Trujillo, la Cárcel Nacional de San Cristóbal y la Cárcel Nacional de Maracaibo, para que varios reos cumplan sus respectivas condenas.
Título de Intérprete Público en el idioma alemán expedido al ciudadano Wolfgang Scherer Gruber.

Ministerio de Minas e Hidrocarburos

Resolución por la cual se declara la caducidad de varias concesiones mineras.
Resolución por la cual se dispone otorgar a la señora Dot Lemon, el título de una concesión minera.
Título de concesiones mineras conferidas a favor de las personas en ellas mencionadas.

Procuraduría General de la República

Sentencia dictada por la Comisión Investigadora prevista en la Ley contra el Enriquecimiento Ilícito de Funcionarios o Empleados Públicos con respecto al ciudadano José Antonio Díaz Villanueva, quien ejerció los cargos de Director de Política y Director de Administración del Estado Carabobo. — (Véase número 837 Extraordinario de la GACETA OFICIAL DE LA REPÚBLICA DE VENEZUELA, de esta misma fecha).

Avisos

MINISTERIO DE RELACIONES INTERIORES

República de Venezuela. — Ministerio de Relaciones Interiores. — Dirección del Ceremonial y Acervo Histórico de la Nación. — Número 1. — Caracas, 6 de febrero de 1964. — 154° y 105°

Resuelto:

El ciudadano Presidente de la República, de conformidad con la Ley ha tenido a bien conferir la Condeco-

ración de la Orden Francisco de Miranda, en su Segunda Clase, al ciudadano Coronel Tomás Pérez Tenreiro, Agregado de las Fuerzas Armadas Nacionales a la Embajada de Venezuela en Roma.

Comuníquese y publíquese.

Por el Ejecutivo Nacional,

MANUEL MANTILLA.

MINISTERIO DE HACIENDA

República de Venezuela. — Ministerio de Hacienda. — Dirección de la Renta Interna. — Número 5. — Caracas, 5 de febrero de 1964. — 154° y 105°

Resuelto:

Por disposición del ciudadano Presidente de la República y de conformidad con los artículos 17 y 18 de la Ley de Publicaciones Oficiales, téngase como oficial la edición de setenta mil (70.000) juegos de formularios RC-1, cuyo precio por ejemplar se fija en cinco céntimos de bolívar (Bs. 0,05).

Este formulario que consta de dos páginas y tres partes, se empleará como comprobante que, anualmente y al cesar en su trabajo, deberán entregar los Agentes de Retención a los contribuyentes correspondientes.

La impresión fue hecha por la firma "Transkrit de Venezuela C. A.".

Comuníquese y publíquese.

Por el Ejecutivo Nacional,

Por Delegación del Ministro de Hacienda,

Benito Raúl Losada,
Director General

MINISTERIO DE FOMENTO

República de Venezuela. — Ministerio de Fomento. — Dirección General. — Número 219. — Caracas, 24 de enero de 1964. — 154° y 105°

Resuelto:

Vista la apelación interpuesta por el ciudadano Henneke Sieveking, de este domicilio, contra la Resolución N° 413, de fecha 10 de junio de 1963, dictada por el ciudadano Registrador de la Propiedad Industrial, por medio de la cual se negó el registro de la marca de fábrica "Glase", para distinguir: alimentos e ingredientes alimenticios, Clase 46.

Para decidir se observa:

Por cuanto la marca de fábrica cuyo registro se solicita puede prestarse a confusión y además tiene parecido gráfico y fonético con la marca "Glaxo", registrada con anterioridad bajo el N° 24.632, de fecha 12 de mayo de 1961, cuyo titular es la firma "Glaxo Laboratories Ltd.", la cual distingue: sustancias alimenticias y sustancias usadas como ingredientes de alimentos, Clase 46, encontrándose por tanto incursa en las disposiciones prohibitivas contenidas en los ordinales 11° y 12° del artículo 33 de la Ley de Propiedad Industrial; se declara sin lugar

natural de Berlín, Alemania, el presente Título de Intérprete Público en el idioma Alemán. —
Caracas: veintinueve de enero de mil novecientos sesenta y cuatro. — Años: 154° de la Independencia y 105° de la Federación.

COPIA DEL ACTA DE EXAMEN DEL CIUDADANO WOLGANG SCHERER GRUBER, ASPIRANTE AL TITULO DE INTERPRETE PUBLICO EN EL IDIOMA ALEMAN

"En la ciudad de Caracas, a los veintinueve días del mes de enero de mil novecientos sesenta y cuatro, se reunieron los ciudadanos: Gudrun Olbrich, Guenther Von Richetti y Adolfo Weisshaar, designados por el Ciudadano Director de Justicia y Registro Público, de conformidad con el artículo 7° del Reglamento de la Ley de Intérpretes Públicos, para constituir el Jurado Examinador del ciudadano Wolfgang Scherer Gruber, quien aspira a obtener el Título de Intérprete Público en el idioma Alemán.
A las 3 p. m., como estaba fijado, y en uno de los locales del Ministerio de Justicia y Registro Público, en el Ministerio de Justicia, se procedió al examen que versó sobre el dominio del castellano y el idioma alemán, con dos pruebas eliminatorias: una escrita y otra oral, durante las cuales el aspirante escribió un folio en alemán que tradujo al castellano, luego otra en castellano que tradujo al alemán, y finalmente, una prueba oral que versó sobre ejercicios de conversación y gramática alemana.
Terminado el examen, el mencionado Jurado, previa consulta y deliberación, resolvió aprobar al aspirante, en virtud de que si posee los conocimientos necesarios para dársele otorgar el Título de Intérprete Público en el idioma alemán, y se acordó entregar un ejemplar del acta al aspirante y dos copias al ciudadano Director de Justicia y Registro Público, a los efectos de Ley. — El Jurado Examinador: (fdo.) Grudrun Olbrich, (fdo.) Günther Von Richetti y (fdo.) Adolfo Weisshaar'. — Hay un sello de la Dirección de Justicia y Registro Público.

COPIA
DEL ACTA DE JURAMENTO DEL CIUDADANO WOLFGANG SCHERER GRUBER, ASPIRANTE AL TITULO DE INTERPRETE PUBLICO EN EL IDIOMA ALEMAN

"Hoy, veintinueve de enero de mil novecientos sesenta y cuatro, ha comparecido ante este Despacho el ciudadano Wolfgang Scherer Gruber, aspirante al Título de Intérprete Público en el idioma Alemán y, habiendo sido aprobado en el examen reglamentario, según consta del acta enviada a este Despacho por el Jurado Examinador, de acuerdo con lo preceptuado en el artículo 13 del Reglamento respectivo, el nombrado ciudadano Wolfgang Scherer Gruber, prestó juramento de obedecer la Constitución y Leyes de la República, y de cumplir leal y honradamente los deberes inherentes a las funciones de Intérprete Público. En fe de lo cual firman: El Director, Rafael Moreno. — El Juramentado, Wolfgang Scherer Gruber". — Hay un sello de la Dirección de Justicia y Registro Público. Se hace constar además, que esta acta aparece asentada bajo el N° 1, folio 170 del Libro de Juramento de Intérpretes Públicos llevado en este Despacho.

MINISTERIO DE MINAS E HIDROCARBUROS

República de Venezuela. — Ministerio de Minas e Hidrocarburos. — Dirección de Minas. — Número 60. — Caracas, 29 de enero de 1964. — 154° y 105°
Resuelto:
Por cuanto la Compañía Anónima "Minas de Níquel Cabrini", cesionaria de las concesiones de níquel y otros minerales de veta denominadas "Cabrin N° 1", "Cabrini N° 2", "Cabrini N° 3", "Cabrini N° 4", "Cabrini N° 5",

"Cabrini N° 6", "Cabrini N° 7", "Cabrini N° 8", "Cabrini N° 9", "Cabrini N° 10", ubicadas en jurisdicción del Municipio Ciudad Bolívar, Distrito Heres del Estado Bolívar, otorgadas a los ciudadanos Fred Goetsch y José Antonio Landaeta Díaz, según títulos publicados en la GACETA OFICIAL número 25.793, de fecha 9 de julio de 1958, ha dejado de pagar por más de un año el impuesto superficial estipulado por el artículo 86 de la Ley de Minas vigente; por tanto, de conformidad con la causal 1ª del artículo 65 de la mencionada Ley, se declara la caducidad de las expresadas concesiones.
Publíquese.
Por el Ejecutivo Nacional,
Por delegación del Ministro,
Julio César Arreaza A.
Director General

República de Venezuela. — Ministerio de Minas e Hidrocarburos. — Dirección de Minas. — Número 61. — Caracas, 29 de enero de 1964. — 154° y 105°
Resuelto:
Por cuanto se han cumplido los requisitos que establece la Ley para el otorgamiento de oro, de aluvión denominado "Cristina 7", constante de un mil hectáreas, ubicado en jurisdicción del Municipio El Dorado, Distrito Roscio del Estado Bolívar, y cuyos linderos, según el plano levantado por el ingeniero Raúl Cabrita Parilli, son los siguientes: se toma como punto de referencia el botalón N° 3, vértice Noroeste del denuncio de oro de aluvión denominado "Cristina 6", de la misma denunciante y que viene a ser el botalón N° 1 vértice Suroeste del presente denuncio; desde este punto, con rumbo Norte franco, se miden 2.000 metros para fijar el botalón N° 2 ó vértice Noroeste; desde este punto, con rumbo Este franco, se miden 5.000 metros para fijar el botalón N° 3 o vértice Noreste; desde este punto, con rumbo Sur franco, se miden 2.000 metros para fijar el botalón N° 4 ó vértice Sureste, y desde este punto, con rumbo Oeste franco, se miden 5.000 metros para llegar al punto de partida o botalón N° 1, con lo cual se cierra el perímetro rectangular; por tanto, de conformidad con el artículo 147 de la Ley de Minas vigente, se dispone otorgar a la señora Dot Lemon, el título de la concesión.
Publíquese.
Por el Ejecutivo Nacional,
Por delegación del Ministro,
Julio César Arreaza A.
Director General

Doctor Manuel Pérez-Guerrero, Ministro de Minas e Hidrocarburos de la República de Venezuela: Por cuanto el señor François Tucek Bevcova, ha llenado las formalidades requeridas por la Ley de Minas vigente, para obtener una concesión de mica y otros minerales de veta, a la cual ha dado el nombre de "Martha II", ubicada en jurisdicción del Municipio La Quebrada, Distrito Urdaneta del Estado Trujillo, constante de cien hectáreas, y cuyos linderos, según el plano levantado por el Ingeniero de minas Carlos A. Freeman, son los siguientes: se toma como punto de referencia el botalón número cuatro de la concesión "Martha" del mismo concesionario; desde este punto se miden quinientos metros, con rumbo Este franco, para fijar el botalón número uno de la presente concesión; desde este punto se miden un mil metros, con rumbo Sur franco, para fijar el botalón número dos; desde este punto se miden un mil metros, con rumbo Oeste franco, para fijar el botalón número tres; desde este punto se miden un mil metros, con rumbo Norte franco, para fijar el botalón número cuatro, y desde este punto se miden un mil metros, con rumbo Este franco, para llegar al botalón número uno, con lo cual se cierra el perímetro rectangular; por tanto, de acuerdo con la Resolución del propio Ministerio, Dirección de Minas, número 1038, de fecha 14 de noviembre de 1963, publicada en la GACETA OFICIAL, número 27.804, de fecha 25 del mismo mes, confiere a favor François Tucek Bevcova, sus herederos o causahabientes, por un período

GACETA OFICIAL

DE LA REPUBLICA DE VENEZUELA

AÑO XCII -- MES XI   Caracas: jueves 27 de agosto de 1964   Número 27.527

SUMARIO

CONGRESO NACIONAL

LA COMISION DELEGADA DEL CONGRESO DE LA REPUBLICA

Considerando:

Que en la mañana del domingo 23 del mes en curso pereció trágicamente, víctima de accidente ocurrido sobre el Río Caroní, un grupo de personas mayorita-

riamente constituido por educadores que en la infausta oportunidad del siniestro asistían a las deliberaciones de la XIX Convención Nacional del Magisterio;

Considerando:

Que esta tragedia no solamente merma los valiosos cuadros de la Federación Venezolana de Maestros y enlutahonorables hogares, sino que afecta sensiblemente el capital moral de la República, por cuanto son los maestros los forjadores del patrimonio espiritual de la Patria;

Acuerda:

Primero: Expresar su solidaridad con el duelo que aflige al Magisterio, a los familiares de las víctimas y al pueblo de Venezuela en general;

Segundo: Dedicar la presente sesión a rendir homenaje a la memoria de las personas desaparecidas y guardar un minuto de silencio con tal motivo;

Tercero: Enviar copia del presente Acuerdo a la Federación Venezolana de Maestros y al Colegio de Profesores de Venezuela.

Dado, firmado y sellado en el Palacio Federal Legislativo, en Caracas, a los veintiseis días del mes de agosto de mil novecientos sesenta y cuatro. Años 155º de la Independencia y 106º de la Federación.

(L. S.)

El Presidente,

LUIS B. PRIETO F.

El Vicepresidente, Encargado,

LUIS PIÑERUA ORDAZ.

Los Secretarios,

HÉCTOR CARPIO CASTILLO.

FÉLIX CORDERO FALCÓN.

PRESIDENCIA DE LA REPUBLICA

DECRETO NUMERO 120 — 18 DE AGOSTO DE 1964

RAUL LEONI,

PRESIDENTE DE LA REPUBLICA,

conforme a la atribución 14 del artículo 190 de la Constitución y al acuerdo de la Comisión Delegada del Congreso Nacional de fecha 12 de agosto de 1964, en Consejo de Ministros,

Decreta:

Artículo 1º.—Se acuerdan, con cargo a las Reservas del Tesoro, los siguientes créditos que en su conjunto ascienden a la cantidad de veintiocho millones cuatrocientos treinta y ocho mil novecientos diecisiete bolívares (Bs. 28.438.917) adicionales a las Partidas y Capítulos que se especifican a continuación del Presupuesto de Gastos vigente del Ministerio de Educación:

Al Capítulo 4 "Dirección Técnica",
Partida 12 "Otros Gastos de Personal" ...Bs.   6.300.000,00
Al Capítulo 5 "Dirección de Educación
Primaria y Normal", Partida 12 "Otros
Gastos de Personal"   4.371.072,00
Partida 20 "Materiales y Suministros"   562.300,00
Partida 40 "Conservación, Reparaciones y Construcciones Temporales"   311.000,00

paso mediante las señales reglamentarias, y ejecutará la maniobra para adelantarse solamente después que haya recibido clara y precisa la señal afirmativa del buque que deba darle paso. En todo caso, la operación no podrá realizarse cuando se encuentre navegando otro buque en sentido contrario y haya riesgo de colisión.

En ningún caso podrá un buque adelantarse a otro en el sector del Canal de Maracaibo determinado en el número octavo de esta Resolución;

d) En los canales ningún buque podrá fondear ni amarrarse a boyas;

e) En los canales no podrán ejecutarse operaciones de pesca.

Cuando en circunstancias de emergencia la operación de fondear tenga que realizarse dentro de un canal, deberán tomarse todas las medidas posibles para evitar que el buque bornee.

Décimo tercero: En tiempo de bruma, lloviznas o fuertes chubascos, o en cualquiera otra circunstancias que limite la visibilidad en los canales, los buques que naveguen por ellos deberán moderar su velocidad, teniendo cuidadosamente en cuenta las circunstancias existentes.

Décimo cuarto: Los buques que tengan que fondear en las proximidades de un canal lo harán de manera de no interrumpir el paso de los otros buques, teniendo en cuenta al respecto el espacio necesario para su borneo.

Décimo quinto: Las infracciones a lo dispuesto en la presente Resolución serán sancionadas de acuerdo con las disposiciones correspondientes de la Ley de Navegación.

Se deroga la Resolución de este Despacho, Dirección de Marina Mercante, Nº 4 de 3 de abril de 1963.

Publíquese.

Por el Ejecutivo Nacional,

LORENZO AZPÚRUA MARTURET
Ministro de Comunicaciones

MINISTERIO DE MINAS E HIDROCARBUROS

Doctor Manuel Pérez-Guerrero, Ministro de Minas e Hidrocarburos de la República de Venezuela:

Por cuanto la señora Dot Lemor ha cumplido las formalidades requeridas por la Ley de Minas vigente, para obtener la adjudicación de una concesión de oro de aluvión, a la que ha dado el nombre de "Cristina 6", ubicada en jurisdicción del Municipio El Dorado, Distrito Roscio del Estado Bolívar, constante de un mil hectáreas, y cuyos linderos, según el plano correspondiente, levantado por el ingeniero Raúl Cabrita Parilli, son los siguientes: se toma como punto de referencia el botalón Nº 1 de la concesión de oro de aluvión denominada "Cristina 5" de la misma denunciante, el cual es a su vez el botalón Nº 1 de la presente concesión; desde este punto, con rumbo Oeste franco, se miden cinco mil metros para fijar el botalón Nº 2, desde este punto, con rumbo Norte franco, se miden dos mil metros para fijar el botalón Nº 3; desde este punto, con rumbo Este franco, se miden cinco mil metros para fijar el botalón Nº 4, y desde este punto, con rumbo Sur franco, se miden dos mil metros para llegar al botalón Nº 1, con lo cual se cierra el perímetro rectangular; por tanto, de acuerdo con la Resolución del propio Ministerio, Dirección de Minas, número 509, de fecha 10 de julio de 1964, publicada en la GACETA OFICIAL, número 27.490, de 14 de los mismos mes y año y de conformidad con el artículo 147 de la citada Ley, confiere a favor de la señora Dot Lemor, sus herederos o causahabientes, por un período de veinticinco años, y siempre que cumplan las disposiciones legales pertinentes, el derecho exclusivo de extraer el mineral indicado, dentro de los límites de la expresada concesión, y aprovecharlo una vez extraído, así como los demás derechos que determina la Ley. — El presente título será protocolizado en la Oficina Subalterna de Registro del Distrito Roscio del Estado Bolívar. — Las dudas y controversias de cualquier naturaleza que puedan suscitarse sobre esta concesión y su explotación y que no

puedan ser resueltas amigablemente por las partes contratantes, serán decididas por los Tribunales competentes de Venezuela, de conformidad con sus leyes, sin que por ningún motivo ni causa puedan ser origen de reclamaciones extranjeras. — Dado, firmado y sellado en el Ministerio de Minas e Hidrocarburos de la República de Venezuela, en Caracas, a los catorce días del mes de agosto de mil novecientos sesenta y cuatro. — Años: 155º de la Independencia y 106º de la Federación.

(L. S.)

MANUEL PÉREZ-GUERRERO.

DENUNCIO MINERO

Ciudadano Registrador Subalterno del Territorio Federal Delta Amacuro.

Su Despacho.

Yo, Ismael V. Fernández, venezolano, mayor de edad, profesor, domiciliado en Caracas, y portador de la Cédula de Identidad Nº 2.154.890, ante Ud. con el debido acatamiento ocurro, de conformidad con el artículo 134 de la Ley de Minas vigente, para denunciar, como en efecto denuncio, un yacimiento de oro de aluvión y demás minerales de aluvión no radioactivos, al cual he denominado "FLOR Nº 1", con una superficie de un mil (1.000) hectáreas, situado en terrenos baldíos en la jurisdicción del Departamento Antonio Díaz del Territorio Federal Delta Amacuro, en la región comprendida entre los ríos Amacuro y Cuyubini, y que se delimita así: Se toma como punto de referencia un botalón de concreto con cabilla en el centro, situado en la parte más alta de la loma de La Ceiba, a corta distancia de la antigua pica balatera de Cipriani y al Sur de la Quebrada Arenal; de allí se miden con rumbo Norte franco un mil (1.000) metros para fijar un poste testigo, del cual con rumbo Este franco se miden quinientos (500) metros para fijar el botalón Nº 1 en el vértice Nor-Este. De allí con rumbo Sur franco se miden dos mil (2.000) metros para fijar en el vértice Sur-Este el botalón Nº 2; De este punto con rumbo Oeste franco se miden cinco mil (5.000) metros para fijar en el vértice Sur-Oeste el botalón Nº 3, del cual se miden con rumbo Norte franco dos mil (2.000) metros para fijar en el vértice Norte-Oeste el botalón Nº 4, de donde se miden con rumbo Este franco cuatro mil quinientos (4.500) metros para llegar al poste testigo con lo cual se cierra el perímetro rectangular y queda así delimitada la superficie de este denuncio. Hago constar que este denuncio, que limita al Norte y al Este con terrenos baldíos, al Sur con mi denuncio de hoy Flor Nº 2 y al Oeste con mi denuncio de hoy Flor Nº 3, no invade concesiones vigentes ni caducas. — Es justicia que espero en Tucupita a los diez y siete días del mes de febrero de mil novecientos sesenta y cuatro.

Ismael Fernández.

Oficina Subalterna de Registro del Territorio Federal Delta Amacuro. — Tucupita, diez y seis de mayo de mil novecientos sesenta y cuatro. — 155º y 106º

Hoy, a las 8,45 minutos de la mañana, en mi presencia y en la de los ciudadanos Petronio Meneses y Rafael Martínez, mayores y vecinos portadores de la Cédula de Identidad números 1.385.125 y 2.776.546, respectivamente; se leyó y confrontó el documento original con sus copias y habiendo resultado fieles, éstas fueron firmadas por su denunciante Ismael V. Fernández, quien se identificó ante mí y los testigos mencionados como mayor de edad, venezolano, profesor, de este domicilio, y con Cédula de Identidad Nº 2.154.890. Hago constar que el anterior denuncio fue presentado para su protocolización hoy a las 8,30 antes meridiem. Quedó registrado bajo el número treinta (30) folios vto. del 41 al 42 del Protocolo Primero del segundo trimestre del año en curso. Los derechos causados fueron los siguientes: Renglón, Bs. 4,55. Derecho Especial, Bs. 100,00. Papel Protocolo, Bs. 1,00. Total, Bs. 105,50.

El Registrador,

E. Marrón R.

we have to clear a small distance with machetes for the jeep to pass."

Dot spent the remaining years of her life attempting, unsuccessfully, to retain control and exploit the "Cristinas" mining concessions. In the end, despite her heroic efforts, a combination of her failing, fragile health, and the nefarious efforts of numerous unsavory schemers and lawyers in Venezuela combined to defeat Dot in her last grand challenge. What remains unknown of this final chapter in her life is an explanation of why, and under what circumstances Dot was granted this extraordinary award of highly valued gold concessions by the Venezuelan Government.

There are several theories. While many aspects of Dot's Venezuela gold adventure remain obscure, it seems probable that her consuming interest in Venezuelan gold came about as a partial result of her long affiliation with and ultimate presidency of the Institute of Navigation (ION), with its roster of highly distinguished scientists and navigation experts. She became close friends, as I mentioned in a previous chapter, with ION founder Capt. P.V.H. Weems and his wife Margaret, as well as with other members of the ION. One of Dot's principal financial supporters for her Venezuelan gold venture was Adm. C.F. Horne Jr. (1906-1990), a prominent member of the ION. It is likely other members of the ION community contributed financial support, although I have been unable to discover any business records of Dot's quixotic Venezuelan gold adventure. Dot's long letters described her life and gold venture efforts in Venezuela, extolling the virtues of the Venezuelan native population and culture, in contrast to much of what she found wanting of the 1960s "hippie" culture in the US. The question remains as to what might have been the role of the ION in the decision of the Venezuelan government to grant Dot Lemon these twenty-five-year gold mining concessions. Why would they honor this unique US citizen with such a concession?

Dot Lemon 1961

As stated previously, the official purpose of the ION is and was as follows: "The Institute of Navigation, founded in 1945, is a non-profit professional society dedicated to the advancement of the art and science of navigation. It serves a diverse community including those interested in air, space, marine, land navigation and position determination." During the 1930s and 40s there were several Venezuelan expeditions, including The Great Savannah Expedition, 17 December 1938, commissioned by Venezuelan President Jose Eleazar Lopez Contreras; the Venezuelan-Brazilian Boundary Commission, 1939-40; 1937-38 Phelps "Venezuelan Expedition of the American Museum of Natural History;" these expeditions were run to delineate borders between Venezuela, Guyana and Brazil and to explore the Grand Savannah, covering many miles of uninhabited jungle and mountainous terrain. These would have been projects ideally suited to draw upon the scientific and navigational expertise of subsequent members of the ION. Had some of its members been involved or studied the results of these expeditions, Dot Lemon, as ION president, would surely have become aware of any official and unofficial reports. Given the terrain involved, transport was highly dependent upon aircraft, instrument navigation, and flying, areas in which Dot was an acknowledged expert. Yet Dot's participation or that of any other ION members' direct or indirect participation in any of these expeditions, remains to be confirmed.

Jimmie Angel

Jimmie Angel, whose on-line Venezuela story in 2006 had originally drawn me to the Dot Lemon quest, was frequently referred to as a soldier of fortune, and a talented bush pilot. His flying expertise was often utilized in support of explorations in the 1930s of the Grand Savannah of southwestern Venezuela, explorations which resulted in greater interest in the region. Workings of the Venezuelan Ministry of Development in association with the American Museum of Natural History, and the Venezuela-Brazil Boundary Commission, resulted in the exploration, cartography and beginning of a systematic scientific evaluation of the vast Gran Savannah. "According to legend, Angel's first trip to Venezuela was in 1921 with an American mining geologist named McCracken. They landed Angel's plane on a mysterious tabletop mountain and removed many ounces of gold. Angel's quest to rediscover that location lasted for the balance of his colorful life."

In 1933 Jimmie Angel discovered the highest waterfall in the world, located in Venezuela and subsequently named "Angel Falls." "The History of Jimmie Angel," Jimmie Angel Historical Project, accessed 23 March 2018, http://www.jimmieangel.org/History.html.[41]

What about Dot and Jimmie Angel? Their names are inextricably linked regarding gold ventures in Venezuela, and Dot's acquisition of the "Cristinas" gold mining concessions. Both Dot and Angel were pilots and former barnstormers whose paths surely crossed, either in the United States or elsewhere. It is said that Angel had a predilection for red-heads: both his wives were red-heads, and Dot had flaming red hair. The Lemon/Angel names are commonly joined in speculation that Dot or an unknown husband of hers accompanied Jimmie Angel when he discovered Angel Falls in 1933, and that upon Angel's death in 1956, Dot somehow became a beneficiary . . . but of whom, and for what reason? This theory connecting Dot Lemon to Jimmie Angel as the reason for Dot's acquisition of the "Cristinas" concessions remains in the realm of unconfirmed speculation. Moreover, Dot's location during the 1932-36 time frame remains unconfirmed. There are only vague references in her letters about gold exploratory trips to Latin America. Moreover, one or more of her alleged sons may have been born in those years. She told stories to the children of a neighbor in California (circa 1960) in which she described "having lived with the Indians."

I have discovered only one known record of contact between Dot and Jimmie Angel. In a letter written by Dot from Ciudad Bolivar, Venezuela to her mining venture benefactors (un-named), dated 13 January 1962, she is describing the difficult terrain in the area. "I now realize why Jimmie Angel, Hugh Morrisy and so many whose names I have now forgotten used to try to explain to me in Florida that they HAD to have a tri-motor Ford or a Fokker Universal, or just anything with two engines, as I should just see what they had to fly over in Venezuela. Well now I have seen. And I must say I am glad I thought so much of Jimmie Angel. I read his eulogy in Los Angeles with respect and affection in my heart." Jimmie Angel died in a Panama City, Panama hospital in 1956.

Another theory would be one linking ION connections to the Venezuelan Government on the basis of unknown services rendered, resulting in Dot Lemon somehow becoming the beneficiary of the Venezuelan government's gratitude for services rendered by the ION. Research in Venezuela on this long-debated mystery has not been possible during the era of President Chavez control there. However, given the reputed great value of the "Cristinas" gold mining concessions, why the Venezuelan Government saw fit to bestow them on Dot Lemon in 1964 surely remains a great story yet to be uncovered. Beginning with Dot's being granted the Cristina gold concessions in 1964, up to the present, the "Cristinas" gold properties have been the subject of continuous multi-million dollar claims and counter-claims by governments and international mining interests. See El Caso Las Cristinas (The Cristinas Case) by authors Alan R Brewer-Carias, Francisco Zubillaga Silva, and Gerardo Fernandez. This book details the long-lasting legal and other efforts to exploit the "Cristinas" gold properties, but Dot Lemon was there from the very beginning.

CHAPTER **15**

Final Puzzle ... Still a Mystery Woman!

DOT LEMON'S MANY varied and notable accomplishments are a matter of record. Still, she remains in part an enigmatic denizen of her largely self-constructed astrological and mysterious world.

Who was her birth father? Why does she start using the Whitney name parentage? Her birth father could have been a member of the Borden family, whose address at 1020 Lake Shore Drive, Chicago she cited frequently. I do not know how or where her birth father met Dot's birth mother Josephine Reque, but her choice of this Chicago address has to have had some meaningful connection. Dot once commented to Roger Dettmer, "You know, I wasn't born behind the staircase!" Did her birth mother work at the Borden residence on Lake Shore Drive as a maid? Could her birth father have met Josephine Reque while he was a guest there? If either of these several possible scenarios were the case, it could explain the source of Dot's financial support for her years at the prominent Bush Conservatory of Music in Chicago, or her claimed law degree from the Albany (NY) Law School.

If Dot had a wealthy undeclared birth father, this would

explain her hints about her origins from a prominent family, yet she repeatedly refused to provide details, saying that this part of her life was "private." Could such an unnamed benefactor have also supported her four boys, whom she claimed as sons yet never fully identified, perhaps due to a pact of anonymity in return for financial support?

What were the circumstances of her birth and subsequent adoption? Who arranged the adoption? Here again the Borden family seems a likely candidate, given its affiliation with the Illinois Children's Home and Aid Society. If Dorothy was a foundling as related by Martin family descendants, found in a basket on the doorsteps of an orphanage, how was her birth mother Josephine Reque identified, and surfaced for purposes of the adoption, according to official records by the State of Wisconsin?

Did Dorothy/Dot have children . . . were they the four boys who are mentioned throughout her history? Were they imaginary or real? If so, who were they, and where are they? What happened to them? Roger Dettmer, who was with Dot on visits to Cincinnati, Los Angeles, and Chicago, over a period of some years, told me she had never revealed details regarding her alleged four sons. According to Dettmer, Dot made a one-time reference to a European plane crash in which a grand-son and family were killed. When Dettmer told Dot he had made inquiries to confirm the event, she became emotional and severely berated him.

(This could have been the event Dot referred to in her August 1973 letter to me in which she told of her "six days of horror for me since the tragedies took place." However, the dates do not correspond. Dot ended the Roger Dettmer relationship in 1967, well before Dot's 1973 episode of grief. I have no other possible explanation for her 1973 period of mourning.) No children were ever seen at Belvedere Field, where Dot lived and worked for at least five years (1935-1940), according to a live, first-person source. If they existed, these would have been the adolescent years of her alleged sons.

There have been numerous newspaper articles referring to Dot as the mother of four sons. This information undoubtedly originated from Dot herself in interviews with the press.

Dot dedicated her book "One-One" to "my eldest son Little Red, lost in the Korean war." Unclassified US Embassy Caracas message no. 07492 dated 5 August 1986, para. 4, states that Dot Lemon had four sons: William, Sherwood, Clinton, and Wellington.

In a personal letter dated 10 September 1964 Dot wrote, "It seemed best at the time not to tell the boys it was BOTH eyes. So, last March, when Clinton's body was destroyed by a drunken American whose car plowed across the road and into him, he still did not know and I am so glad now I did not tell him. He worried enough about my health as it was." Here Dot was referring to having gone legally blind from, according to her, an overdose of sulfa drugs and peritonitis, circa 1953.

Finally, Dot's letter to her close friend in April 1964 made yet another written reference to her possibly fantasized sons.

While I have had many wobbly moments over whether the boys really existed, the hard truth is that I have discovered no verifiable third party instances of any one actually seeing them. We do know that Dot had a fertile imagination. She often alluded to her Danish ancestry, including vague references to "Queen Christina." In fact, it appears Dot knew the name of her Norwegian birth mother "Reque" having included that name as part of her alleged Whitney mother's maiden name.

There is one more tantalizing element in Dot's often obscure life story. Yet another unknown ...in the form of fleeting references to an inconspicuous, yet not insignificant, man in her life. In a one-line sentence in an undated letter, Dot says she went with "McCoy" to see Cinerama at the New Orpheum Theater in San Francisco," probably in the 1950's. In an earlier letter

Dot wrote she attended a performance at the American Ballet Theater in Cincinnati with Bill McCoy, after which they were at an after performance party at the home of Charles Taft (son of former US President,) likely in the late 40's or early 50's. Then, in a letter dated April 1964, Dot talks about McCoy saying "he went home last Sunday and I have been ill ever since. He really does take a lot out of me ... it wasn't always this way, but when I told him a few years ago that I couldn't marry him, he changed and went into his shell and since then it's been awful for him and I've been sick about it but that's the way it is and I can't help it." (Dot's only documented legal husband, William Richard Lemon, died 20 March 1964.) Then, in a letter dated 4 May 1969 written from Venezuela, Dot says "McCoy died last year and I was executor of his will and had to stay up there four months as they had already stolen one-half million out of his estate by the time I got there." This puts McCoy's year of death in 1968, and Dot's likely four months in the US dealing with his estate in late 1968 to early 1969. It seems unusual, at a minimum, for a non-family member to be executor of the will of a deceased person.

While this relationship between Dot and McCoy appears to have been a long time semi-intimate one, efforts to identify McCoy have been extensive and unsuccessful. McCoy also may have been a financial contributor to Dot's "Cristinas" gold venture in Venezuela.

Finally, how, and under what circumstances did she acquire the gold concessions in Venezuela? Dot's title to the "Cristinas" gold concessions properties is a matter of official Venezuelan record. A verifiable explanation remains one part of the Dot Lemon saga yet to be unearthed.

Epilogue

GIVEN DOT'S UNIQUE real-life record of accomplishments, this heroic adventure story is truly remarkable, revealing elements of fantasy, philosophy, true grit, and mystique. I remain in substantial agreement with Roger Dettmer, the former prominent music critic of the Chicago Tribune, who said the following about Dot in a piece he wrote for the jacket of Dot's book "One-One." "When I first met Dot Lemon it was at once and overwhelmingly evident that here was my candidate for 'The Most Unforgettable Person I've Ever Known' award. The interim years have served chiefly to strengthen that indelible impression, and to firm my vote as quite possibly 'The Most Unforgettable Person Anyone Can Ever Know.'"

So, who was Dot Lemon, really? The final details of her possible family origins and life remain one of history's potentially most fascinating stories. Who should get credit for her gifted and acknowledged intellect, added to her pioneering efforts and accomplishments in many fields of endeavor? Why did she never acknowledge the circumstances of her humble birth, illegitimacy, and Norwegian parentage? Much of her self-invented Danish heritage seems likely to have constituted a personal mythology in denial of her actual birth circumstances. My personal great regret is that my friendship with her from 1971 to 1973 only exposed me to her waning years of failed health and mental deterioration. Yet her story has led me over the years on an intriguing life experience, for which I owe a debt of gratitude to Dorothy... or Dot, and whoever else she may have been.

She was a truly remarkable woman that made a number of advances for women in an era of the male-dominated world. Dot Lemon deserves to be listed among the outstanding women characters and aviators of the 20th century.

Why not call her the original "Lean-In" lady!

References

1. Book inscription to Richard Kinsman by Dot Lemon.
2. Dot Lemon letters to author, dated 8/21/1973 and 9/9/1980
3. Dot Lemon personal letter to Margaret Weems, 11/24/1963
4. Brink/Lemon Marriage License #7858, State of Florida, 4/4/1937
5. Dot Lemon affidavit dated Jan 6, 1942 affirming marriage to Leon Brink at Rochester, NY October 18,1927; also affirming divorce from Brink March 10, 1937 in W. Palm Beach, Florida; also affirming marriage to William Richmond Lemon on April 4, 1937 in W. Palm Beach, Florida.
6. United States Census, 1930, Leon P. Brink
7. United States Census, 1930, Dorothy C. Martin
8. United States Census, 1910, Albert A. Martin
9. Fern Marguerite Martin; Family History/Anecdotes
10. News article by Kenneth Stratton "A Pencil Sketch of a Pilot."
11. Department of Commerce Application for Pilot's License No. 94310, June 1, 1937
12. Syracuse Herald newspaper, July 23, 1929
13. "Women With Wings," Charles E. Planck, Harper & Brothers, 1942
14. Enslow History, Ancestory.com
15. "City Aviatrix Gets Global Award," Oklahoma City Times, Jan. 8, 1948
16. Florida Department of State, Division of Corporations, W.R. Lemon Inc.
17. United States Department of State, UNCLASS CARACAS 07492, 051649ZAUG86.
18. Dot Lemon personal news letter page 9, dated September 10, 1964.
19. Dot Lemon personal letter to the Lunts family, April 5, 1964.
20. Dot Lemon Social Security Application (263-05-7463) dated Dec. 5, 1936.
21. Dot Lemon Birth Certificate #97862 (copy) dated Nov. 21, 1941.
22. Dot Lemon affidavit dated Jan.6, 1942 certifying a true copy of her birth certificate #97862 showing her DOB August 22, 1907, Cook County, Illinois, and Whitney parentage.
23. Contemporary Authors, Gale Research Biography
24. Bush Conservatory of Music, 1920's
25. Department of Commerce Application for Pilot's License #91029, Sept. 22,1936.
26. Milwaukee County Court Order For Adoption, Oct. 8, 1907.
27. Miami Daily News Record (Miami, Oklahoma) Aug. 1, 1943
28. United States Census, 1880, Albert A.A. Whitney.
29. San Antonio Express (San Antonio, Texas) Feb. 2, 1947.
30. Daily News Standard, Uniontown PA., Feb. 14, 1933.
31. Dot Lemon personal letters to her family, dated August 1942.
32. Civil Aeronautics Authority Application, 1942.
33. Department of Commerce, Civil Aeronautics Administration, Airman Rating Record, Jan. 30, 1945.
34. Charles Tupper Associates, April 3, 1949.
35. International Women's Air & Space Museum (IWASM) "Dot Lemon Curse of an Aviatrix," 2011,12.

36. Dot Lemon book "One-One" book jacket comment by Julliard School of Music composer, Vittorio Giannini.
37. Dot Lemon book "One-One," About the Author, p153
38. Institute of Navigation (ION), 1961-62.
39. Dot Lemon, First ION Woman President
40. Official Gazette (Gaceta Oficial), Republic of Venezuela, Feb. 6 and Aug. 27, 1964.
41. "Jimmie Angel Historical Project," Karen Angel.
42. Dot Lemon and the "Beguine" Cover; National Air and Space Museum, Smithsonian Institution (SI 2006-25056) "Houston International Air Speedrun"

Acknowledgments

THIS BOOK WOULD not have been completed nor complete without the advice, encouragement and contributions of numerous friends, aviation enthusiasts, and Martin/Reque family members. Among the organizations whose members have provided valuable material are the Institute of Navigation (ION), the International Women's Air and Space Museum (IWASM), The 99's, and the Norwegian American Genealogical Center-Naeseth Library (NAGC-NL).

Two Martin family descendants, Donna Martin Elliott and Mary Salvo Abendroth kindly shared family archives material absolutely critical to this story. To them I am most grateful. Krista Reynen, a professional researcher, accomplished much original searching. Jorge M. Gonzalez helped with Venezuela knowledge and history. John Reque and Jarle Rekve (in Norway) of the Josephine Reque genealogical line generously shared time and family knowledge. David Reade, a professional author and journalist, shared Dot Lemon historical timelines from his early Lemon research. Sue Dodds, of the Weems family, shared family letters and material. John Underwood, an aviation guru and writer, with encyclopedic knowledge of the field, provided critical research and assistance on many occasions. John Turley, a neighbor, friend and writer, provided guidance and encouragement when most needed.

SEARCHING FOR DOT LEMON

Finally, my wife Sheila, and children Robin, Richard and Ted were always available with much needed editing, computer knowledge and patience over the many years of this effort. To them I owe much.

CPSIA information can be obtained
at www.ICGtesting.com
Printed in the USA
FSHW021213110519
58059FS

9 781732 619104